T0208270

Born with a Veil

Living with the Unliving

Ruby Aline "Lane" Baker

authorHOUSE®

AuthorHouse™
1663 Liberty Drive
Bloomington, IN 47403
www.authorhouse.com
Phone: 1 (800) 839-8640

Published by AuthorHouse 07/18/2019

ISBN: 978-1-7283-1996-4 (sc)
ISBN: 978-1-7283-1997-1 (hc)
ISBN: 978-1-7283-1998-8 (e)

Library of Congress Control Number: 2019909983

Print information available on the last page.

This book is printed on acid-free paper.

INTRODUCTION

"Born with a veil" is a term given to a baby who is born with a thin layer of skin over his or her face or body. Although it is rare, it does happen. The skin must be removed upon the baby's birth. According to the older generation, a child born with a veil can see and hear things others cannot. She or he had to learn quickly to expect the unexpected and to live with the unliving.

This book is the story of the life of one such child born with a veil. It also tells the experiences of other family members who have also seen and heard things that cannot be explained.

CHAPTER 1
Reminiscing the Younger Years

As I sat on the front porch of my modest apartment and stared at the clear, blue sky, I began thinking how fast the years had gone by. I turned seventy this past birthday, and looking back, I see this little girl who was hit with a lot of big problems that seemed unfair for a child to have to have faced.

My parents had two daughters and wanted a boy, but I came along and made their third daughter. I was just another girl. I remember a lot of love and attention going on and especially the love between my mom and dad.

We lived in Valdosta, a small community in Tuscumbia, Alabama. Tuscumbia is part of the Shoals Area, sometimes called the Quad Cities. The Shoals Area consists of four cities in north Alabama so close together that you can't tell when you leave one and enter the other except for Florence. The Tennessee River separates Florence from Sheffield, Muscle Shoals, and Tuscumbia.

We lived behind the Valdosta Church of Christ; a big field separated us from the church. Mr. Bendall did some farming there in the summertime, but we still walked across the corn and cotton fields to the church services, where Gilbert Kretzer, a kind and intelligent man, was the minister.

My sister Brenda was my best friend; she took care of me in all kinds of ways even though she was just a little girl too and only eighteen months older than I was. I remember her taking up for me against other kids in the neighborhood, and I remember when I was sick how she would sit with me, hold my hand, and stroke my curly blond hair until I fell asleep. She and I would play outside all day, and a lot of times, I heard piano music playing right beside us. I would say something about the beautiful piano music, and Brenda would say, "I don't hear a piano." I would have a strange feeling; I couldn't understand why I could hear it so plainly and she couldn't hear it at all.

Our sister Dot was already going to school and Brenda would tell me often that she would be starting school soon. I knew I wouldn't be able to get through the day without her. "Please, Brenda, please don't go to school," I begged.

"It'll be all right, Aline. I won't be at school very long," she said.

The day came too quickly for Brenda to start school. Oh, how I missed my sister every day so much. I would hang out on the swing, climb the trees, and kick in the dirt. I was so lonesome, and it sure seemed like a long time to me.

Dot, the oldest, was four years older than Brenda and six years older than me. Brenda and I were no more than a nuisance to her—two younger sisters whom she would have preferred had never been born. She liked being the only child and didn't mind telling us so. She told us often that she wished we had never happened. Dot was spoiled, and all the kids in the neighborhood spoiled her. When they played ball, she had to always be the captain, choose her team, and bat first—and she was never out.

Mother was a hardworking mom. She would build a fire outside under a big, black wash pot and put the laundry in. She would stir the boiling water with an old broom handle. She would scrub each item on a rub board and then rinse and hang them on the clothesline to dry. She canned vegetables in the summer; she let us kids wash the Mason jars that she put the vegetables in, and then in her spare time, she would read *True Story* magazines.

Mom became in the family way again, and she and my dad were still hoping for that boy. My daddy was the apple of my eye; he was *my dad.* He worked hard at Reynolds Aluminum and rode the work bus. Our house was in seeing distance of the bus stop, so when it was time for the bus to bring him home, his cat, Ol' Tom, and I would go there and wait. He would let us ride home sitting on his shoulders, me on one shoulder and Ol' Tom on the other. He was a good dad and a good husband who loved his family.

Dot taught me how to run from Daddy when we were going to be disciplined for doing something we knew we were not supposed to do. "If you run from Daddy and can run faster than him," she said. "He'll start laughing and stop running, and then you won't get that whipping." I was so scared to try what Dot said to do; I was scared I couldn't outrun him, but the next time it happened, I ran, and it really did work.

Grandma came to live with us, and Grandpa went to live with his other daughter since he was ill and needed her to care for him. Grandma was the boss. She was highly respected by everyone in the house.

Dot taught me how to sit in the tree and make faces at Grandma. One day, we did something that Grandma didn't like, so we ran outside with Grandma chasing us. Dot said, "Hurry! Hurry, Aline! Climb the tree! Grandma's too old to climb, and she can't reach us up there." So we climbed the tree, sat on a limb, and made faces at her while she stood there asking us to come down. But we kept laughing and making ugly faces. Grandma said, "Okay, girls, the hoecake will get you." Then she turned and went back in the house.

We sat there on that limb for a long time playing a game called

Ritter Ma Ritter Marie, I See Something That You Don't See. We knew when we came down that we would get a whipping for making those faces. It was in the summer, and the windows were all open. We smelled something delicious. That good aroma kept coming straight to us and smelled better and better, so we came down. It was that hoecake Grandma had told us about, and it did get us. After the whipping, we got a piece of that delicious corn bread she called hoecake.

CHAPTER 2
Dead, Ghost, and Warning

One day, Grandma and I were the only two at home, and she was sitting by the window rocking in her favorite chair—the one no one was ever allowed to sit in; it was Grandma's chair. Grandma motioned to me and said, "Aline, come over here and look at what I see." I looked out that big window and saw a woman walking down the Old Lee Highway. We watched as the woman turned into our long driveway.

"Who is that, Grandma?" I asked.

Grandma said, "That is my sister Lizzy, but Lizzie is dead."

This woman dressed in black was standing there in our driveway right where Daddy always parked the car. Then suddenly she was gone. I was not yet of school age. I was too young to understand what had just happened, but I was scared. Somehow, I knew this was not anything normal and should not be happening.

Grandma said, "Aline, I don't believe in ghosts, but I do believe in warnings, and what we just saw was a warning."

I was scared and didn't really know why; I didn't really know what it meant to be dead. *Dead, ghost,* and *warning* were new words for me. I really didn't understand. I thought I would just wait until Brenda got home from school and see if it scared her; I would ask her if she knew what those words meant. After all, she was a second grader, and I thought she knew everything.

That evening, a brother of Grandma's came to our house to tell her that their other brother had died. Grandma turned to me and said, "I told you, Aline. What we saw today was a warning."

It wouldn't be long until I would be six and would go to school. That scared me too. Brenda said going to school was a good and fun thing to do, but I was still scared.

The summer was a fun time; I had Brenda to play with all day. We played hard from sunup to sundown and sometimes fell asleep at the dinner table. Then Daddy would carry us to bed. I felt so safe in his arms; I felt so loved as he tucked us in.

The summer seemed so short. I had to go to school. Dot made sure I already knew the alphabet and how to spell a lot of words and knew most of the first-grade arithmetic. Brenda held my hand and walked me all the way to my room, saying, "It's going to be all right, Aline. It's going to be all right. School isn't so bad. Lots better than staying at home with no one to play with."

Before the day was over, I really did like being at school. My teacher, Miss Olive, was a kind person and was really impressed with the things I already knew. In a few days, she drove me home from school telling me she needed to talk to my mother. I was wondering all the way from the Valdosta school to our house, *What did I do?*

When Mama opened the door, she looked surprised to see my teacher with me. "Come in, Miss Olive, and have a seat," Mother said. "Tell me what brings you here."

Miss Olive sat and said, "I would like to put Aline in the second grade. She already knows everything I would be teaching her in first grade."

Mother thought for a minute and said, "No, I really don't think that would be good. I would rather she was in the grades with children her age."

"Well, it's up to you, Mrs. Howard," Miss Olive said.

They talked for a while and shook hands; Miss Olive left.

That week brought more excitement. "It's time for me to go to the hospital," Mother said to us kids, "and we'll bring the baby home with us."

Grandma and us girls stayed on the front porch and watched as Daddy helped Mother get in the car, tossed her overnight bag in the back seat, got one leg in the car, and turned and said to

Grandma, "Mrs. Black, please make sure that my babies have plenty of milk to drink."

"I will, Clay," she answered. She said to Dot, "I wonder why your daddy said that. We always have milk."

I was so happy that day thinking it wouldn't be long and we would have a real baby to play with. And maybe—just maybe—it would be a boy.

Grandma left to visit with her brother. Brenda and I were playing with our baby dolls. Dot was ironing Daddy's white shirt so he would have it to wear back to the hospital to get Mama and the baby. There was a knock at the door; Dot opened it, and there stood two of Mama's favorite nieces, Judy and Bertha. When Brenda and I noticed they were outside with Dot, we went out there too. They were saying something to Dot, and I thought I heard that word again—*dead*. I had forgotten to ask Brenda what that meant. Dot started crying hard; she ran inside to the bedroom with me and Brenda running right behind her. She threw herself across the bed, so we did too. Still sobbing, Dot said to us, "It's Daddy. He had a heart attack. Daddy's dead."

We were all three crying, but I still didn't understand why. I was crying because Dot and Brenda were crying.

Later, Brenda explained to me exactly what it meant to be dead. "It means Daddy stopped breathing and won't be coming home. He's gone to heaven to live with Jesus," she said. "We have a spirit inside of us, and if we stop breathing, our spirit goes to heaven, and they put our body in a hole in the ground. That's what dead means."

That was still not very clear to me; it sounded scary.

"The baby won't be coming home either," she said. "It's a boy, but he's dead too."

Then there was the funeral for Daddy and the baby Mama named after him, Clay Washington Howard Jr. There were lots of people crying. There was much stuff I didn't want to think about; I just wanted my dad to hold me and ride me on his shoulder.

Glen View Farm delivered milk to our house twice a week, so Grandma started paying the bill telling Mother that she had made the promise to Clay to make sure his children always had milk to drink.

A few months later on a bright, sunny day, Mother sent Brenda and me to Uncle Ned's, the neighborhood store, for a loaf of bread. We kicked pebbles all the way to the store and left them outside so we could kick the same ones back home.

About halfway home, I saw Daddy walking toward us. He was in front of the Valdosta Church of Christ. He was dressed the way he had liked to dress—in his overalls and a white shirt with the sleeves rolled up. I stopped kicking my pebble and started running to him. Brenda was yelling at me, "Where are you going, Aline? Come back here, Aline!"

I thought my dad had not gone to heaven—he was right there. I kept running, but just as I reached him, he was no longer there.

Crying and pulling on Brenda's dress, I screamed, "Where did he go? Where did Daddy go?"

"No one was here," she said. "Daddy wasn't here."

"I saw him, Brenda. I really saw him!" I said.

As soon as we got home with the bread, I asked my mother, "Why did I see Daddy and Brenda didn't?" She thought for a minute and started to cry. Through her tears, she answered, "Your daddy isn't here. He died, and now he's in heaven. If you saw him, that has to be a warning."

"What does warning mean?" I asked.

"Warning means something bad is going to happen," she answered. "I don't believe in ghosts, so this has to be a warning."

That was the same thing Grandma had said, but I didn't hear of anything bad happening.

CHAPTER 3
Life Goes On With Unwanted Visitors

Life had to go on even without Daddy. Mother had never worked a regular job before; she had worked only part time at the dime store a few weeks at Christmas time. Mother got a job working at Robbins Floor Products making floor tile. It was a good place to work, and she met friends and started going out, doing things for herself and us that she had not done before. We got a telephone, a washing machine, and a refrigerator, and we got our house painted on the outside and inside.

In a few years, Mother met Robert Wallace and married again. Dot, being fifteen, had married Curtis Willis. She and Mother were expecting babies. Mama had another girl and named her Sheila, and five months later, Dot had a boy they named Clay. That was okay. I loved the new babies very much.

Sheila became my baby in a lot of ways. Mother was having

problems with Robert's drinking; he would sometimes take off from work for a couple of weeks to go on a drunken binge. Mother went back to work to keep us all fed, so Brenda and I had to be the mother to the baby and keep the house going. I was ten then; I would grab the baby, the bottle, and the diaper bag and go play with my friends. They were a little envious of me; I had the real baby and theirs were just dolls.

When the babies began to talk, Sheila and Clay had problems saying "Aline." It sounded like they were saying "Lane," so with that, I became Lane to everyone except Brenda.

One time, I was in the orchard getting enough apples for Brenda to make us the apple pie Mother had taught her to make and suddenly I heard Grandma groan. I looked around and saw her lying on the ground. I ran to her and asked what was wrong, but she couldn't talk, so I ran in the house yelling for Dot. "Dot! It's Grandma!" I screamed. "She's on the ground, and she can't talk."

Curtis and our cousin, O'Neal Behel, were there, so they all ran to her, picked her up, put her in the car, and rushed to the hospital. Grandma had had a stroke. A few weeks later, she passed away. The funeral was a sad time; Brenda and I held each other and cried. I wondered how we were going to get by without the boss, the one who had kept us out of trouble.

We grew up way too fast. We had no choice; that was just the way it was, and we all had to pitch in and do our part.

One time when Brenda and I were riding our bicycles past the orchard, I saw this old woman wearing a gorgeous, long white dress with pink roses and a long white apron standing at a peach tree about six trees away. She looked like Grandma. I stopped my bike and ran to her. When I got closer, I saw it was Grandma. I yelled to Brenda, "Look, Brenda! It's Grandma!"

Brenda stopped her bike and ran to me; she took my hands, looked straight in my eyes, and said, "Aline, I don't see anyone."

I turned around. Grandma was gone; she wasn't there. I still couldn't understand why I saw and heard things Brenda couldn't.

In a couple of years, Mother had taken all she could stand with Robert's drinking and finally saw her lawyer. She got a divorce and started another life without him.

Time passed quickly; Brenda and I were attending Cherokee Vocational High School. She and I rode the bus from Valdosta to Cherokee, a small town just outside Tuscumbia.

When Brenda was almost sixteen and I was fourteen, she started dating, so it wasn't long before I started dating too. I went to school one day while she played hooky. That morning, she just didn't want to go, and if Brenda didn't want to go to school, she didn't go. When I got home from school, she said, "Aline, I met these two good-looking guys today, and I made a date for you for

Saturday night with Frank Baker. I'm going with his friend, Larry Filyaw."

"And just what does this Frank look like?" I asked thinking she was probably playing a joke on me and setting me up with an ugly creep since we sometimes did things like that to each other just to be funny.

"I said good-looking guys, didn't I?" she answered.

Saturday night arrived. I had been nervous all day doing my hair, getting my best dress ready, and preparing for this date. I was hoping he was as much as Brenda had said he was.

We heard a car pulling into our long gravel driveway; two guys got out. My heart was racing; I could hardly breathe. Looking out the window, I saw this handsome guy with black hair who was the driver of this gorgeous turquoise-and-white '56 Chevy and hoped he was Frank. "Brenda, which one is Frank?" I asked.

"The one with dark hair is Frank. Larry's the blond," she answered without looking.

After that, my first date, I just knew this was the guy for me, and I hoped he would someday feel the same as I was feeling then.

I was only fifteen and Brenda was seventeen, but since we had to grow up so fast, we were more like twenty-year-olds. After Brenda and I dated Larry and Frank for almost a year, Mother gave in and signed for us to marry. Brenda and Larry married one month and Franklin Delaneo' Baker and I were married the next month. Frank was twenty-five, but he was just right for me; my grandma had always said she would rather be an old man's darling than a young man's slave.

Mother was working and living in Florence, so she let us have her house, and we would watch Sheila for her. Frank and I were so in love, and I was trying hard to be a super-good wife. I would have the house clean and supper cooked every day by the time he got home from working hard on his construction job. I made sure I was looking good when I met him at the door with a kiss. It wasn't long until we were talking about having a family of our own though we had Sheila, who was almost five then.

"How many kids do you want, Frank?" I asked.

"Oh, I don't know," he said. "Maybe about five—two boys and two girls. The fifth won't matter."

Frank started driving a big rig that sometimes took him out of town for the night. When he was going to be gone overnight, we would leave Sheila with Dot, and he would take me with him. It was exciting sitting in the big truck watching him handle the traffic and pulling out when I thought he should wait, but he would just laugh and say, "That little car ain't gonna hit this big truck."

Every month, we kept hoping for a baby, but it just wasn't happening. I went to Dr. Bentley, who said, "Lane I can't find anything wrong with you except that you're young and you may not be completely developed."

We waited for another year, and I returned to the same doctor. That time, he suggested that Frank be tested. When the test came back, the doctor told him his count was low, but it didn't mean he couldn't have children; it meant that it might take longer than usual.

We still had Sheila, so we were doing what most parents did—making sure she had a good place to call home, sending her to school, loving her, and tucking her in bed at night.

When Sheila was seven, Mother married Hershell Comer, whom everyone called Red because of his red hair. He was the best stepfather anyone could ever have, and Sheila went to live with them. Red drove a bus for Mars Hill Bible School, so they enrolled Sheila there. She said riding Red's bus was exciting; she liked watching him pick up and deliver all the students.

Frank and I bought our first house; my sisters threw us a surprise housewarming party with lots of family, friends, and gifts. By then, we were faithful members of and taught classes at the West Side Church of Christ. I was working as a beautician but not liking it at all. Frank was a night-shift supervisor at a factory making hinges and hasps for the ammunition boxes they were using in the Vietnam War.

I wanted a job at the factory so badly. At first, Frank said that it wouldn't be a good idea, but finally, he consented and got me hired on the night shift. He liked being my boss, and he really tried to make an example out of me by not letting me get by with anything—not one thing. He would say, "If I let you get by, I'll have to let everybody get by," so I did whatever he said to do.

Betty Black, a very sweet cousin, had had rheumatic fever and whooping cough when she was very young; it had settled in her lungs. She was only twenty-two, but she was not doing well. She coughed a lot; her bronchial tubes and lungs were deteriorating. She became very sick and was in the hospital on life support. One time when Dot and I went to the hospital to visit her, Linda, her sister, came out of Betty's room in tears. "Betty passed away," she said.

Betty's sister Cathy was there; she looked out a window, and through her tears, she said, "I just saw Betty floating up in the sky."

It was so sad to know that my cousin, my friend, was no longer here.

It was a nice funeral. When I got home, I thought about how we had been friends even as children; we had had Easter Egg hunts at our house. When I was a child, I thought Betty and Linda's mother, Stella, made the best Easter eggs I had ever tasted. I wanted to keep the housewarming gift Betty had handmade for me forever. I opened the dresser drawer and took out the gift, which was still in the gift box. It was three pieces of fruit made with fabric to hang on the kitchen wall. I gently picked up the fruit, held them close to my heart, and through my tears, I told her that I loved her and that she was already missed. I put the gift back in the drawer.

That evening after Frank left for work, I lay down to get a nap before I had to go in to work at eleven. I fell asleep quickly. I was awakened by someone coughing continuously. I jumped out of bed and looked all around the room and then all over the house, but I couldn't find out where the coughing was coming from. It was a hard cough, and it was close to me no matter where I went in the house. It sounded just like Betty's cough. I went from room to room calling Betty's name. I was terrified.

My neighbor called and said, "Lane, your attic light is on."

"Thanks, Mildred, for letting me know," I said.

I went up to the attic, and the coughing was there too. "Betty, if you're here, please show me or give me a sign that it's you," I said. I couldn't remember ever being that scared. I turned off the light and went downstairs. The coughing stopped. One light at a time started going out. The house was dark—all the lights were off.

I reached into a kitchen drawer for the flashlight Frank kept there and turned it on. I went to the phone hanging on the kitchen wall by the back foyer. I called the emergency number for the electricity department just to be told that my electricity should not be off, that I should check my fuse box. I did what they said, and it didn't appear anything was wrong with it, so they suggested I call the police because someone had to be outside messing with the power.

The police came, but even they could not find any reason for the power being off. They checked the power box, and it was fine. I was still nervous and scared even with the police and their big flashlights; it was so spooky standing there in the dark house.

The lights came on just as suddenly as they had gone off. The police said, "You need to get an electrician to come and check your wires tomorrow."

By then, it was time for me to get dressed for work. I had to rush or Frank would not be happy with me. I jumped in the car and headed to work. It seemed to be extra dark on the road that night, and I was still spooked with all that had happened. And then the coughing started again. I looked over to the passenger side where the sound of the cough was coming from. There sat Betty with a bright glow surrounding her; however, she was not like herself—she was almost transparent. I knew what that meant; I was scared, trembling, and so terrified that I pulled the car over to the side of the road.

Crying, I begged, "Please, Betty, please don't do this!"

She smiled a sweet smile and vanished. Still crying, I pulled back on the road and sped to work as fast as I could hoping I wouldn't be late.

I didn't see Betty anymore, but the coughing persisted at home. My neighbor called to say, "Lane, your attic light is on again."

"Thanks, Mildred. I'm so sorry you have to keep letting me know. I don't know what I'm going to do about this light."

"It's okay, Lane. I know you'd do the same for me," Mildred said.

I went up to the attic and switched the light off.

After visiting with my aunt Ruby and telling her about Betty and how she appeared to me on my way to work, Aunt Ruby said, "Maybe she wants you to take the gift she made for you out of the drawer and hang it on the wall."

"Well, Aunt Ruby, you may be right," I said.

When I got home, the coughing started as soon as I walked in. I went to my dresser and got the gift box. I took out the three pieces of fabric fruit and hung them on the kitchen wall. They looked gorgeous hanging over the table. And the coughing stopped immediately. I was at peace knowing Betty had made the fruit and had put her heart into every stitch. I think Betty was at peace too.

I never heard the coughing again, and the attic light never came on again unless we turned it on.

Things at the factory were slowing down since the war was beginning to end and a lot of our military men were coming home. I was one of the last hired, so I was one of the first to be laid off.

I wasn't one to sit at home, so I went back to my old job at the beauty shop. That meant I had to start getting up early again, which wasn't my ideal thing to do.

My favorite patron was my sister, Brenda. She came in early one morning, and I told her that ever since I started having to get up early, I was getting nauseous and sick at my stomach. She laughed and said, "You're probably allergic to early hours." We laughed at that, but before she left, she said, "You should go see your doctor. Maybe he could give you something for your stomach."

So I went to Dr. Mims about the very sick feeling I was having, and he turned me over to Dr. Bentley, who gave me an exam and said, "Lane, I have some good news for you."

"Let me have it. I need something good," I said.

He smiled. "Lane, you and Frank are finally going to have that baby."

I was so excited. As soon as Frank came in from work, I blurted out, "Frank, I went to the doctor today and we're going to have a baby!" I saw the shock on his face.

"What? Did I hear that right?"

"Yes, you heard it right!"

We were so excited that we were really going to be a complete family after eleven years. After a few hugs, Frank went straight to the bedroom and closed the door. I put my ear to the door. I heard him saying on the phone, "Guess what, Mama? We're finally gonna have a baby!" He was so happy. I didn't think I had ever seen him that happy.

Not long after that, Frank was laid off from the factory, but it wasn't long before he got a job working out of the carpenters' local. However, his first job sent him out of town to Atlanta. From Sheffield, Alabama, to Atlanta was quite a distance, so that meant he had to stay all week and come home on Friday nights for the weekend. Frank's friend, Leon Britnell, got a job there also, so they traveled together, shared a motel room, and became even better friends.

Sheila came to stay with me so I wouldn't be alone. Things seemed to go so fast with me working at the shop and waiting for Frank to get home every Friday. Then it happened; I gave birth to a baby girl we named Deedra Joan. She weighed only five pounds and was born very sick with asthma and allergies. I took off from work for the first four months after Deedra's birth to care for her. When I went back to work, Sheila watched her.

A year later, Sheila got married, and it wasn't long until she was expecting her first baby. Her marriage didn't last, so she moved back in with us before her baby was born.

Red, our precious stepfather, was sick due to a war injury to his lung; he was in the VA hospital in Memphis. The odds were against his coming home. I was with him as he was dying. He pointed to the ceiling and asked, "Hey Lane, what are they doing up there?"

"Who, Red?" I asked.

"Those angels," he said.

I didn't know what to say because I didn't see any angels.

He said, "Lane, I know I won't get to see Sheila's baby, but will you tell her that I will love the baby with all my heart?"

"Of course I will, Red."

I never heard his gentle voice again. His death was devastating to the family; he had been a gift from God and the best thing that had happened to our family since my dad.

In a few months, Sheila gave birth to a girl she named Misty. Misty also was born with asthma and sometimes had a hard time breathing.

It had been a while since the incident with Betty, so I had not thought about scary things in a long time.

We fixed up a little area of Deedra's room to be the nursery; we had twin beds on one side of the room and a crib for Misty on the other side. One night, I had just put Deedra in her bed and I was sitting on the edge of the other bed folding diapers. The lights flickered. There on the other side of the doorway standing in the foyer was this dark shadow the size of Red. I was again so scared; the memory of Betty came back as I watched the shadow move slowly toward the crib. I watched in amazement as the shadow leaned down over the baby as though to kiss her. It slowly rose and floated back through the doorway and into the foyer—then it disappeared. My heart was jumping. With tears running down my face, I grabbed the baby and took Deedra out of her bed. I held them close not wanting anything to happen to my babies.

The following day, I went to see my mother and told her about the shadow I had seen. "Mother," I said, "I think it was Red, and I think he was there to see Sheila's baby. It looked as though he leaned down and kissed her. I don't know why these things have to happen to me and seem to always be when no one else is around."

My mother said, "Lane, I haven't wanted to tell you this, but I think now's the time for you to know."

"Know what, Mama?"

"You were born at home with a veil over your face. Doctor Loren Gary took you to the window so he could see better and clipped it off."

"What's a veil, Mama?"

"It's a thin layer of skin that grows just inside the hairline and falls over the face and looks like a veil."

"What does this have to do with me seeing a shadow, Mama?"

"The old folks say that people born with a veil have special powers and have the ability to see and hear things that others can't see or hear."

"What do you mean, Mama? Are you saying I can see those who are dead?"

"Yes."

I caught my breath. A feeling of being different came over me. I didn't want to be able to see the dead; I just wanted the dead to rest in peace and leave me alone. I erased the special-power thing from my mind; after all, I had Sheila and the babies with me.

The carpenters' local sent Frank and his friend, Leon, to Chattanooga to work on erecting a nuclear plant; at least that was a little closer than Atlanta.

Within a year, Leon became sick with lung cancer, and it wasn't long before he passed away.

One night a few weeks later, Sheila took Deedra and Misty to visit with their grandma, and I was alone trying to get the house clean. I heard very hard, loud knocking on the back door. Everyone used the back door as an entrance since our driveway was at the rear of the house. Thinking it must have been Sheila with the babies, I stood my mop in the corner and rushed to the door. I opened it, and there in the darkness stood Leon Britnell. Thinking I just couldn't go through this again, I yelled in a trembling voice, "Go away, Leon!"

That scary image of Leon looked so dead. Without blinking an eye, he stretched his words as he mumbled, "I wantttt toooo seeee Frankkkkkkkkk."

"You're dead, Leon. You can't see him. You're dead. Go away!" I screamed.

The image of Leon slowly faded. I slammed and locked the door and hurried to the phone. I called Mother and told her as calmly as I could, "Tell Sheila to come home. It's the kids' bedtime."

We talked for a minute; I ended the call with "I love you, Mother."

"I love you too, Lane."

CHAPTER 4
Home Sweet Home

When Deedra was two, Frank and I decided we needed to sell our house and move to Chattanooga. "That will be good, Frank," I said. "But what about Sheila and Misty?"

"We'll help her get an apartment for her and the baby and get her a phone. Since she's working, they'll be okay."

We were so happy when our house sold in only eight days and we were on our way to Chattanooga to be the family we desired so much to be.

We bought a new mobile home and found a private lot out in the country just outside Chattanooga in a small place called Ooltewah. The lot was on a hill and surrounded by trees. It was a perfect place for Deedra to have a swing set, a sandbox, and a nice shady place to play. This was going to be our home sweet home.

We were so happy. Frank was working the night shift, and I

was taking care of Deedra and the home. I made sure I had a good dinner cooked and waiting for him when he got home at midnight. We had lots of time in the day to play with Deedra and do family things that we had had to neglect for some time. We decided to clear some of the trees in the rear of the lot to make more room for Deedra to play and to put up a barbeque grill Frank wanted.

While we were clearing the lot, we noticed it was connected to a cemetery, and that didn't make me happy. We took a walk through the cemetery, which was creepy and full of old graves. "Frank, I wonder why there are no new graves here."

"Probably because it's full."

"Let's go. I don't like it here," I said.

"Oh heck, Lane. There isn't a thing to be scared of. These people can't hurt you. They just make you hurt yourself."

We hurried home, where I felt safe. Frank had never experienced anything out of the ordinary, so he wasn't a believer of the supernatural or spirits. He said that there was always an explanation for everything. He even had his doubts about the things I had seen.

We had a good weekend putting together the swing set we got Deedra for her third birthday. Frank was flipping burgers on our new grill as I pushed Deedra in the swing. "Higher, Mom, higher!" Deedra would say in her little girl voice laughing, and enjoying every minute of having her mom and dad together enjoying the family life she had been so deprived of.

"I'll never leave y'all again," Frank said. "If I have to go, we'll all go together—that's a promise."

I didn't think life could get any better than that.

After that amazing weekend came a horrible Monday. Deedra's asthma was really giving her some problems, and I remembered what my mother had done for Brenda and me when we were little and had asthma. Old Doctor Gary, our family doctor, had told her to put us in the sun without our tops on and let our lungs bake in the sun. I—a good seamstress—made Deedra a lot of bikini swimsuits, so she had one for every day of the week. I started lying in the sun to get a good tan for the summer, and I would put Deedra in a bikini; she would have fun in the sandbox.

On that day, I put my swimsuit on and put Deedra's bikini on her, and we went outside. I had my blanket, my radio, my Coppertone lotion, and my book, *Thirteen Alabama Ghosts*, which Sheila had given me for my birthday. I spread my blanket and set my radio to my favorite country music. We were ready to meet the hot sun. I was lying on my stomach reading when I felt something on my leg. Thinking it was just a fly or moth or something harmless, I shook my leg, but it didn't leave. It was actually crawling up my leg.

Being frightened of anything that wiggled, I jumped up just

knowing it was some kind of creepy crawler. What I saw was a nightmare. There were giant locusts everywhere—all over my blanket, crawling all over the mobile home, and all over the yard. I ran for Deedra. She was crying, jumping up and down, and screaming, "Mama! Mama!" Locusts were all over her sandbox.

I picked her up. The locusts were hopping all over us as I was trying to get in the door. When I finally made it inside, one locust was hanging onto my swimsuit. I grabbed one of the flip-flops I was wearing, knocked it off, and stomped it as hard as I could hoping it wouldn't take but one stomp. I picked it up with a paper towel and placed it in a plastic bowl, which I covered with a lid. I wanted to show it to Frank when he got home.

I was still so scared that they would find a way in. I saw them outside crawling all over every window, and I prayed, "God, please make these ugly creatures go away!" I had never seen anything as ugly before, and I didn't know why we were suddenly invaded with them.

They eventually left, and I gave Deedra her bath for the night. After I took a bath, I checked the windows again—the locusts were still gone. I fed Deedra and settled down to watch Deedra's favorite program, *The Six Million Dollar Man*. She had a serious little-girl crush on Steve. She fell asleep, so I carried her to her bed at the end of the trailer. I started dinner for Frank. I decided to make corn bread and beef stew that I would simmer until he got off at midnight. After I vacuumed and put a load of laundry in the washer, I got comfortable and watched *I Love Lucy*. I thought Lucy and Ethel were hilarious as usual.

The night passed fast, and Frank came through the door. "Ummm," he said. "What's that I smell? Oh, I know. Don't tell me. It's that stew I like so well."

"Yes it is, but it'll cost you," I answered.

"How much?" he asked laying a five-dollar bill on the table.

"More than that," I said picking up the five.

He reached for me, pulled me to him, and kissed me with one of those kisses that always melted my heart. "That's enough," I laughed. "That's exactly the pay I wanted, and I'll keep the five thank you very much."

I loved him so much; it was a pure pleasure to fix the things he liked and watch him eat as if it were his last meal.

After he ate, I reached in the cabinet drawer where I had put the bowl and set it on the table. "What is this?" Frank asked with a surprised look on his face.

"It's a nightmare," I answered. I told him what had happened to us after he had left for work. "This just wasn't natural Frank," I said telling him how scared Deedra and I had been.

He just couldn't understand how bad it really had been. "Oh, Lane, it's getting to be summer, and we do live in the country. So do crickets, grasshoppers, and even some snakes," he said as he popped the lid off the bowl. "Wow!" he said. "It looks like it was some big locust! I've never seen one this big. I'm not sure exactly what it is." He got up from the table and took it outside to get rid of it. I didn't ask where because I really didn't want to know.

The next day was a Saturday, and we had planned a cookout and spending time with Frank's little princess. Frank started getting things ready to light up the grill. "Tonight, we'll surprise Deedra and take her to Lake Winnepesaukah," he whispered.

"Okay," I whispered back. "That sounds good to me. I won't say a word."

Lake Winnepesaukah was an amusement park on a lake; the place had a lot of kiddie rides, and it was Deedra's favorite place to go.

Before Frank could even get the grill going, a noise started coming from the cemetery. The noise got louder and louder; it made me want to cover my ears as if I had been too close to a loud siren.

"Let's go see what's going on," Frank said taking Deedra by one hand and me by the other. We walked into the cemetery, where I had said I would never go again, but I wanted to see what the noise was. I saw locusts—big, ugly locusts—everywhere crawling all over every tombstone and all over the gravel road. They were jumping everywhere; some tried to jump on us.

Frank picked up Deedra and started to run. I started running too not wanting him to leave me behind. Once we reached our lot, he sat Deedra down but was still holding her hand as if he didn't want to ever let her go. "I've never seen anything like that," he said still panting.

"I told you, Frank, but you just couldn't comprehend how bad it really was," I said.

"I can now," he said as we were going up the steps.

"We'll just get something to eat at Lake Winnie," Frank whispered, so we got ready and headed out to the amusement park. Frank told Deedra, "We have a nice surprise for you." She smiled, and she stayed as quiet as a mouse in the back seat, but as soon as we rounded the curve on the road that went to the lake, she recognized where she was and started jumping and yelling, "Lake Winnie! Lake Winnie!" She was so excited. What joy it was to see how happy our little girl was.

She rode every ride in the kiddie land. We ate corn dogs and cotton candy and walked all over the park letting her see the lights blinking and flashing in the night. We became tired, so we headed home.

On the way home with Deedra sitting in the middle, Frank reached for her and put her in his lap. "Daddy's little girl wants to drive," he said.

"Frank, don't do that. You're scaring me," I said.

"Oh heck, Lane, you're scared of everything," he said. "There ain't no traffic right now. We're the only ones in sight."

He put her hands on the wheel and took his hands off telling her to keep the car on our side of the white line. There we were going down Interstate 75 under the influence of a three-year-old. I must admit she did pretty well keeping it between the lines. She really was his little girl. When he saw car lights in the distance, he took control of the wheel, and I relaxed.

The next week went well. I didn't think about anything bad or scary. A friend we had gone to church with at the West Side Church of Christ in Sheffield, Alabama, Marie Fleming, called; they were in Chattanooga visiting her sick mother at the Erlanger Hospital. I told Frank that I wanted to bake a cake and take it to the hospital so the family would have something to snack on since they were sitting with her day and night. He thought that was a great idea and said he would watch Deedra.

When I returned home, he told me that Deedra had been swinging on her swing and had come running into the house telling him she had seen me. He said, "I told her that you weren't here, that you had gone to the hospital, but she argued that you were by her swing."

As he was telling me this, she came into the kitchen and said in her little girl voice, "Mommy, I saw you outside." Not yet knowing her colors, she said, "You look like dat all over," pointing to the black blouse I was wearing. "Mommy, I say hi, but you not say hi to me."

"Honey, that wasn't me," I said. "It must have been a neighbor or someone just walking by."

"No, Mommy, no," she said. "It was you. It was you."

Frank started tickling her to get her mind off the subject and said, "Maybe you would like some of that chocolate ice cream we have in the freezer."

"Yes, yes, ice cream!" she said with excitement forgetting all about what she had been trying so hard to explain.

The next night, things got quiet, so I went to check on Deedra in her bedroom. I saw her sitting on the bed with a big pocketknife. The bedspread had slits cut all over it; it was not like our little girl to ever do anything that bad. I asked, "Honey, why on earth did you do that to your gorgeous bedspread?"

She answered in her little girl voice, "Mommy, da lady."

"Where did you get the knife?" I asked. "And how did you open it?"

"Da lady. Da lady," she answered.

I took the bedspread off and put a blanket on her bed. I put Deedra in her bed, turned her TV on, and kissed her goodnight. I took the open knife to the kitchen and laid it on the table for Frank to look at when he got home from work.

When he got home, I showed him the knife and the bedspread.

"This knife is mine," he said. "I had it in my top drawer, so how could she get it, and how could she get it open? It's a very strong knife and not easy to open."

"I don't know, Frank," I answered, "She told me it was the lady."

"It's just not like her to do this. I know she couldn't open this knife," he said.

I knew Frank was concerned, but he didn't mention it again. After that incident, life became normal for a while. Sheila called me and told me that she had gotten married again and that her new husband was Jimmy Daily. A few weeks later, she called to say she was going to have another baby. She told me it wouldn't be long until she would graduate from college; after the baby was born, she and Jimmy would come with the baby and Misty to Chattanooga and get a job.

"Don't wait that long," I said. "Come now for a visit."

"Maybe we will in a few weeks," she said.

After hanging up, I started thinking about how long it had been since we had seen her and Misty, and I wished they could come right away.

Autumn was beginning to set in, and the leaves were beautiful. All of Chattanooga was beautiful. The mountains were so colorful that people were coming from far and near to take the color tour of one of God's best creations.

One day when Frank was at work and I was studying my Bible, I heard a baby cry; it sounded like a newborn, but there were no babies around. I heard footsteps. I thought the crying must have woken Deedra. I kept watching for Deedra to come up the hallway, but she never did, so I put the Bible down and went in her room to see why she hadn't made it to the living room. It wasn't her; she was still fast asleep. A chill went up my spine as I started hearing the baby cry again. *This isn't supposed to be happening. There's no baby here*, I thought.

Then all the lights went off. I reached in the bed and got Deedra. All I could do was feel my way to the sofa, lay Deedra down, and wait for Frank to come home at midnight. We had only the one car. *Another car sure would be handy right now*, I thought. Scared to death, I made my way to the kitchen to where Frank kept a few tools in one of the drawers and felt for the flashlight and a candle. I took a lighter from the drawer, lit the candle, and made my way back to the living room. It would still be another hour before Frank would get home.

The crying continued, and the footsteps sounded like someone was running through the trailer. I heard the *swish-swish* of the carpet, and it gave me an eerie feeling. *Maybe I should take my baby and sit outside*, I thought. I opened the front door, but it was so dark outside that I decided to stay inside. I prayed, "Oh my God, please be with us at this horrible time. Please keep us safe until Frank can get here." I was on the sofa with my little girl hoping she would not wake up to all this darkness and strange noises.

I had never in my life been so happy to hear a car. Frank opened the door and asked, "What on earth are y'all doing sitting in the dark?"

"The lights went out, and I've had a bad experience," I answered.

By then, the battery in the flashlight was getting low, so the light was dim, and the one candle was almost gone. The lights flickered then came on. "Thank goodness," I said. Taking a deep breath, I got up and took Deedra back to her bed.

"Something's strange about this place," I told Frank, "something I can't explain, but something's definitely not right."

Frank just looked at me as if to say, *Oh no, not again*, so I didn't finish what I was about to say.

After Frank ate and took a shower, we settled down on the sofa to watch a good show before going to bed. He had his feet resting on the coffee table, and I was lying with my head in his lap. He said, "Here comes our little girl," when he heard the same footsteps I had heard earlier. We waited, and again, she never got to the living room. He slid out from under my head and went to her room. He came back and said, "That wasn't her. She's still asleep, but I could have sworn I heard footsteps."

"That was the bad experience I was talking about," I said. "Earlier tonight, I was hearing footsteps and a newborn crying. I too thought it was Deedra, but it wasn't her."

"That's so strange," he said. He sat, and I laid my head on his lap. We continued watching the movie.

In the morning, I thought about how I had wished for a car the night before. "Frank, do you think we can afford another car?" I asked. "I really think I need one being here at night all alone and Deedra being sickly. We never know when I might need to get her to the hospital."

"I'll look around and see what I can come up with," he answered.

That Saturday, we were sitting at the table sipping coffee when Deedra came from the living room crying. I put her on my lap and noticed her long hair had been cut very short from the front to halfway around the back. "Look, Frank!" I said showing him her hair.

"How did you cut your hair?" he asked.

Through her tears, she answered, "Da lady, Daddy, da lady."

I went to the bathroom cabinet and got the scissors I used at the beauty shop; I gave her a full haircut. We searched all over the mobile home for the long hair that had been cut off, but we found no hair at all.

Sheila called saying she and Misty would be there on Friday. "Yea!" I said. "Y'all be careful on the road and stay safe." I was so excited. I picked Deedra up and swung her around telling her Sheila and Misty were coming.

"Sissy and Missy are coming?" she asked with excitement. She had always called Sheila Sissy, and I guess she thought she was since she had been around ever since she was born. "Yes, Sissy is coming," I said.

On Monday, Frank came home from work; he had bought a used car from a man he worked with. He said he would use it for his work car and I could have the new car we had purchased just before moving to Chattanooga. It made me happy knowing I would not be stranded again. If something strange happened and I needed to leave, I could. I would rather be sitting in the car in Zayre's parking lot than sitting in the dark trailer listening to footsteps.

Friday finally arrived, and we heard Sheila's car coming up the driveway. We rushed out to meet her. It had only been a few months since we had seen them, but it seemed like a lifetime. Sheila stepped out of the car. I hugged Sheila and reached and took Misty, then age two, from the car. She and Deedra headed for the swing set. It was going to be a good week I thought. "Look at you, Sheila," I said, "expecting again."

"Yep" she answered, "due in April, and for the last time I hope."

I made a good dinner that night especially for her. It had been a while since she had eaten my chicken and dressing she liked so much. I also made the mac and cheese and creamed potatoes, a favorite of the kids. We enjoyed dinner and put the rest in the oven to save for Frank.

I put the kids in the bathtub, and Sheila looked for something interesting to watch on TV. I got the kids dressed for bed, and we tucked them in for the night.

When we were about halfway through the program she had selected, she looked at me and said, "I hear a baby, and it's not one of ours."

"I know," I said. "I hear it too, and I've heard it before. I don't know where it's coming from. The other trailers close by are empty."

"No, no," she said, "this baby sounds like it's right here in this trailer. This would scare me out of my wits."

"That does scare me," I said, "but just wait till you hear the footsteps."

"Footsteps?" she asked, "I don't wanna hear any footsteps."

"Well, if you stay long enough, you will," I said. "Even Frank has heard the footsteps, and every time we hear them, we think Deedra is awake and on her way to the living room. We wait for her just knowing she's coming in here, but when we go check, she's still in bed and sound asleep."

"Gosh," Sheila said. "What the heck is going on?"

"I don't know," I answered, "but it's creepy. Sometimes, I think this place is haunted."

Then we heard the footsteps. It sounded just like someone running through the trailer. "Oh my stars!" Sheila said. "This place is haunted. I sure wouldn't want to live here."

I was so glad she was with me. "You don't think this is a warning that something is wrong with my baby, do you?" she asked.

"I hope not," I answered.

The week went by much too fast; she and Misty were getting ready to leave. We knew we were going to miss them so badly, and the hugs brought on the tears. We waved as far as we could see them.

CHAPTER 5
A Neighborly Visit

We bought a new stereo, and Frank hung the speakers on the wall. I enjoyed the stereo especially when I was cleaning. The country music somehow made the cleaning seem easier and go faster.

Soon after, a family moved into the trailer on the next lot about half an acre away with a barbwire fence separating that lot from ours. I intended to go over to welcome them to the neighborhood as soon as I got a chance.

That night, a storm was coming up. The wind was howling through the trees, and I saw streaks of lightning in the distance. I was cleaning the trailer and doing the laundry and had not turned the stereo on, but every time I passed the speakers, I thought I heard voices. Turning the vacuum cleaner off, I went over to the speakers. I heard the speakers breathing the words "Dieee, diee, die." At that very moment I was startled by a knock at the door.

I opened the door, and there stood a woman holding her jacket closed. Her long, dark hair was blowing in the strong wind. "I'm Vickie, your new neighbor," she said.

"I'm Lane," I said. "Please come in. My husband is at work."

"My husband's at work too, and my two kids are in the bed, so I won't be staying long," she said as she came through the door. "I just wanted to meet you."

"I've been meaning to come over and welcome y'all to the neighborhood. Please have a seat," I said.

As soon as she stepped in, we heard the weird voice coming from the speakers. Not saying a word, she walked over to the stereo and saw that it was turned off. She said to me as she was going to the door, "Lane, you're welcome to come over to my place and stay until your husband comes home, but I'm getting out of here. Those speakers are saying 'die.' There's something bad going on here."

I saw she was frightened. I was spooked too, but at the same time, I was glad I wasn't the only one hearing that.

"Thank you so much for the offer," I said. "I'll come over as soon as I get my daughter out of the bed."

She didn't wait for me. I realized she had never experienced anything like that.

I got Deedra out of the bed, slipped her house shoes on, and wrapped a blanket around her; we walked over to Vickie's.

She was holding the door firmly with the strong wind trying to take it from her. "Come in," she said, "before that wind blows you away."

We stepped inside. "You can put your daughter in my bed if you like," Vickie said, "or she can lie on the sofa."

"I'll just lay her on the sofa," I said. I sat on one end and put Deedra on the other with her head resting in my lap.

Vickie said, "I have coffee already made if you'd like a cup."

"I would," I answered. "That sounds good."

Vickie went to get the coffee. It was going to be a while before Frank would get home. The wind was still howling, and in the trailer, it sounded even worse than it was.

Returning with the coffee, Vickie handed me a cup and sat in the chair opposite the sofa. "This has to be a horrible night for you," she said. She started telling me about how her grandmother had lived in a haunted place. We talked a long time about the things her grandmother had experienced. She had a lot of stories to tell. "I think your trailer is haunted too," she said.

"There's something going on," I said not really wanting to tell her everything I knew.

She said, "My grandmother said she knew someone who had been born with a veil over his face, and he could see spirits."

Just then, I heard Frank drive up; I was happy he was home. I sure didn't want to tell Vickie about the veil I had been born with. "Frank's home," I said getting up and picking Deedra up. "I better get out there and fix him something to eat."

"I enjoyed the visit. We'll do this again," Vickie said as I was leaving.

"Yes, we will," I said.

"Frank!" I yelled out into the darkness as Frank was getting out of his car. "Come here and take Deedra for me."

It was always so dark out there in the country at night. Having no street lights made me miss the city.

"What in the world are you doing out here in the dark this late at night?" Frank asked as he was taking Deedra from my arms not knowing I had been at the other trailer.

"Let's get in out of this wind," I said holding the door open so Frank could get in. He took Deedra straight to her bed. I removed her shoes. We tucked her in with a goodnight kiss and returned to the kitchen. I tried to come up with something quick to fix for Frank's midnight dinner.

"Okay," Frank said, "tell me why you were out on a night like this, and tell me where you've been."

"Frank," I said, "I'm thinking something is haunted about this trailer, and I think I'd really like to move. I miss living in the city, and I don't like living in a trailer. Everything sounds so much louder than it really is, like when it's raining."

"But why were you outside?"

"Well, tonight, the stereo speakers were talking, so I went out to the next trailer," I replied. I told him about the speakers and Vickie's visit and how she was scared and didn't stay even long enough to sit down. "The stereo wasn't on, Frank. There wasn't even a record on the spool," I said.

"I can't understand what it could have been," he answered, "but you know that CB radios are doing things nowadays like coming through the TV, and you may hear their conversation."

"No, Frank, it wasn't a CB. The stereo wasn't on," I said.

Frank checked it out and I looked in the fridge for bacon to make BLTs.

"I don't know what could have caused it," Frank said as he was sitting down at the table to wait for his sandwich. "We can't just up and move. It would take a while to sell the trailer."

I cleaned up the kitchen while Frank was taking a shower. We turned the TV on and watched Johnny Carson's *Tonight Show*. Then it happened again.

"Here comes our little girl," Frank said, and again we waited as we listened to footsteps and the rustle of the carpet even above the wind. Then the baby started to cry. We looked at each other not liking what we were hearing. I got up and checked on Deedra and returned to the living room saying, "Enough is enough. I've stood just about all I can stand. Maybe we could get a psychic or a medium to come out and get rid of whatever's going on."

"How do we contact a psychic?" Frank asked. "It's not like they advertise."

"I don't know, but someone should know. We can ask around and maybe someone can tell us."

I asked Vickie, the girl in the next trailer, but she didn't know one. Frank asked the men on his job, but they didn't know of a psychic either.

A month or so went by, and things seemed to be settling down, so we were back to enjoying our late-night time together. *Red Skeleton* ended with "Good Night and God Bless," so we went to bed to get ready for the next day. We planned on taking Deedra to the adjoining woods to choose a cedar for a Christmas tree, something we had not done since we had been kids. We wanted Deedra to know what it was like to enjoy Christmas the old traditional way.

The tree we chose was beautiful. Frank chopped it down, sprayed it for insects, and left it outside for a few minutes to air out. I popped popcorn, and we made popcorn ropes and twined them on the tree. We baked cookies, threaded them with red ribbon, and hung them on the tree along with candy canes. Deedra was so excited. That was her first Christmas to get to help with the decorating. *Maybe these strange things can leave us alone and we can have a good Christmas*, I thought.

Frank asked an electrician at work if there was any way the speakers could pick up a CB radio even if the stereo wasn't on, and he had told Frank the power wouldn't be there if the stereo wasn't turned on; he didn't think it would be possible for a CB to come through the speaker of a stereo under any conditions. He asked Frank where he lived, and Frank explained exactly where our trailer lot was, on a hill just off Interstate 75 at the Ooltewah exit.

The man said that he knew exactly where it was and that years ago, a trailer parked there burned and a woman and her baby had died in the fire.

It was going to be a good Christmas; we were going to Tuscumbia, Alabama, and have Christmas with our family. It was a family tradition to have a family dinner with everyone bringing food and gifts, and it was always my job to make the turkey and cornbread dressing. I cooked the turkey all day and made the dressing and got everything ready for the three-hour trip. Things seemed to be peaceful then. We had not heard the baby or the footsteps for a while, so we were not going to think about it; we were just going to enjoy Christmas.

As soon as Frank came in from work, he took a shower while I packed up the car. Deedra grabbed her baby doll and was all ready to go; she was so excited about getting to see her grandmother.

We had a good trip singing Christmas carols and laughing, and we even nibbled on the turkey that was all wrapped in Reynolds wrap and resting in the big turkey pan on the back seat. We were so relaxed and happy; I thought it would have been nice if that moment could last forever.

Mama met us at the door with hugs for everyone even though it was in the wee hours of the morning when we arrived.

It was a happy Christmas. The dinner had gone well, but the highlight of the holiday was watching Deedra's and Misty's expressions when they woke up in the early morning and hurried to see the Christmas tree. They didn't care about Santa or who Santa was then; they just wanted to know if the pretty wrapped presents under the tree were for them.

The holiday was over, and it came time to kiss my mother goodbye. She was always sad at such moments, and I hated to see her cry. "Mother, please come and visit in the spring," I said.

"I will," she answered with tears in her eyes.

Back at home, we were getting back to life without having any strange happenings. Nothing had happened for a while, and we were enjoying that. It was nice to just sit and watch our favorites on TV, pray together, and go to bed without thinking about the supernatural.

The spring was warming things up, and the buttercups were everywhere. Wildflowers were covering the hillsides, and we started doing some of the things we had been planning all winter. That was the happiest time of my life. We had such fun checking out Chattanooga; there was Ruby Falls, Rock City, and all of Lookout Mountain to explore and lots of fun stuff to do.

Mother came to visit and brought her sister, my aunt Ruby, with her. I really wanted them to enjoy the visit, so I cooked them a nice dinner every night while they had fun playing cards. During the day, I took them to see some of the sites and for drives around Chattanooga to see the beautiful, breathtaking views.

When the time came for them to leave, I was satisfied that they had had a good time, and I was glad Aunt Ruby was with her. She was so much fun to be around, and she always kept everyone laughing.

Sheila's baby was born—Jim was a cute little thing and looked just like his dad, who was so proud and showed endless love for him. I thought maybe it wouldn't be long before they moved to Chattanooga.

One Saturday morning as Frank and I were sitting at the table drinking coffee, there was a knock at the door. "Who on earth could that be?" Frank asked.

I answered the door, and there from Tuscumbia, Alabama, was my cousin Peggy, her husband, Tom, and their little four-year-old twins, Lorey and Corey. I was so surprised but so happy to see them. They had started on a trip and were passing through

Ooltewah, so they stopped to visit. Frank had always liked Tom and liked being around him, and Peggy was one of my favorite cousins.

"Where's the rest of the crew?" Frank asked since they had three other children, Pam, Bud, and Randy.

"Mama's watching them," Peggy answered, "and getting them off to school."

"What would we do without our mothers?" I asked.

"I don't know," Peggy said. "Mine helps me a lot."

Frank and Tom were busy catching up, and the kids were playing and having a good time. Then it was time to say goodbye and let them continue their trip. I hoped they would stop again on their way back home.

That was a good Saturday. We decided to take a road trip through the beautiful mountains and stop for dinner just outside Knoxville. After we ate, we decided to head back to Ooltewah.

When we got home, we put Deedra to bed, put on our night clothes, and sat on the sofa drinking Pepsi, listening to our country music on the stereo, and talking about how we really liked the Chattanooga area. Then it started up again—the running in the trailer. We hoped it was Deedra, but when she didn't arrive, we looked at each other, and Frank said, "Here it is again."

I was so irritated that the noises had ruined our night. I got up and went outside and cried and begged for this thing to please stop and leave us alone. Sometimes, I thought this thing was surely going to drive me insane and I would be stuck in the Moccasin Bend mental hospital.

When Jim was three weeks old, Sheila brought him and Misty to stay with us while she went out looking for a job. It didn't take long for her to find a good job at the Chattanooga Public Library, so she saved her money, and Jimmy came up and found a job working construction. They moved to their own place a few miles away. We were going through a quiet period again, and it was nice not to have to put up with any scary, eerie, unnatural things.

A few months later, Sheila and Jimmy were not getting along, so Jimmy went back to the Shoals and Sheila and the kids moved in with us. They shared Deedra's room, and I watched her kids while she worked.

It wasn't long until Sheila and Debra Keith, a friend she worked with at the library, started going out on weekends and leaving the kids with us. Debra was a sweet girl and had been raised by very good parents, who lived on Signal Mountain, a few miles from Chattanooga. Debra would sometimes spend the night with us if the weather was bad. It was hard having three kids with the oldest being only three, but we did the best we could and loved each one as our own.

Brenda visited us a few times, and I loved seeing my best friend, but I always hated to see her go when the visit was over.

Dot and Curtis with their kids, Denise and Chris, and their dog, Ol' Rebel, paid us a surprise visit as they were on their way to Kentucky, where Curtis was working on a job with TVA. We talked about Clay being in the Marines and stationed in California and everything that was going on back in the Shoals. The Shoals would always be our hometown. It was always good to have visitors from home.

Oh, what a gorgeous day we awoke to; it was going to be a fun Saturday. We were taking our three kids to different things on Lookout Mountain. Jim was such a sweetheart, and there was this weekly show on TV called *The Waltons* with a boy named John whom they called John Boy. It just seemed natural to call our little Jim, Jim Boy. Jim Boy, Misty, and Deedra had a lot of fun on the mountain, and when nighttime came, they were so tired. We gave them baths and tucked them in for the night; we kissed each one and told them we loved them. We settled back and watched our favorite programs on television.

About midnight, we too were tired, so the bed was very inviting. I fell asleep in Frank's strong arms feeling the comfort of being safe and loved. I was awakened by a strange noise I had never heard before. This noise was a fire. The trailer was on fire! The noise was the crackling of the burning wood. The whole end of our bedroom was burning. I saw the bright red and yellow flames that engulfed the dresser. The smoke was making it impossible to breathe. "Frank!" I screamed. "Get the kids!" I yelled as I was climbing out of bed and grabbing my clothes. Frank saw the flames and jumped out of bed to get into his pants. Then as suddenly as it appeared, the fire disappeared. It was gone. There was no fire! No fire at all.

"Okay" Frank said, "that's it. We're outta here. We're not even gonna think about it. We're not staying here any longer."

CHAPTER 6
Time for A Change

As soon as it got day, we packed our clothes and just the necessities. We got the kids into the car and headed out. We left all the furniture not really knowing where we were going, but anywhere was better than there.

We got a newspaper and found an apartment that would lease to us on the spur of the moment, so we stopped on the way and bought an old used bed from a used furniture store and a can of spray paint. We painted our bed that day, and that night, we made pallets for the kids on the floor. At least we were out of that godforsaken place.

We went to Sears the next day and purchased a black leather living room set and two large beautiful pictures. The pictures were Spanish; one was a handsome bullfighter and the other was a beautiful dancer. Frank hung the pictures over our new sofa. The bright colors in the picture brightened up our living room.

Things were normal; we even began to enjoy our lives and not having to think about what was going to happen next. I got a job at Olan Mills Portrait Lab printing film on the night shift so I could be with the kids during the day and Frank could be with them at night since he was then working days.

I wondered how long the peaceful life would last. I didn't want to think about the weird stuff that I had already suffered, and I hoped it would never happen again. One day as I was cleaning the living room, I stood admiring the beautiful pictures for a moment. I looked at the bullfighter, and it looked to me as if his eyes moved. I went to the kitchen to wash the dishes, and when I finished, I headed back to the living room to finish with the dusting. I glanced at the bullfighter, and his eyes had turned in the opposite direction. I stopped suddenly and told myself it was just my imagination, so I dressed and waited for Frank to get home, and then I left for work.

After that, I saw the bullfighter's eyes move many times, and each time, it was so creepy; it would cause me to tremble and beg for it to stop. I tried hard not to look at this picture. I told only Frank and Sheila about this strange picture; thank goodness, the children never noticed the moving eyes.

One night after work, I invited my friend Carolyn to follow

me home and have coffee with me. I told her I had just made an orange cake that day, which we could have with coffee. She said, "That's a deal, Lane."

We got to the apartment, and I went to the kitchen to make coffee and slice the cake. We were talking and laughing in the dining room having a good visit. Carolyn told me the cake was delicious. Then she said, "Lane, I hate to tell you this—I know you're going to think I'm nuts, but the man in that picture just turned his eyes to look at me."

"Carolyn, I don't think you're nuts," I said. "I've heard of a lot of strange things in my life."

Nevertheless, Carolyn finished her coffee and said she had to go.

Sheila moved back to Tuscumbia and went to work with TVA at a good job. Mother watched her kids while she worked. Frank and I missed the kids, but they were Sheila's, so we had to let go, and we were happy Sheila was being the parent the kids needed.

Several years had gone by since the fire at the mobile home, and we were living a normal life. Frank was working at building every nuclear plant in the Chattanooga Carpenters' local territory, and I was still working at Olan Mills.

My mother went into the hospital with what she thought was the flu, but she was diagnosed with lung cancer, and Frank had been injured on the job.

"As soon as I get my compensation check," he said, "we'll move to Alabama so you can help care for your mother."

We waited and watched the mail every day wishing for that check. In a few days, Deedra came back from checking the mailbox waving the envelope with the TVA address at the top. It was the check. "I knew we'd get it," she said. "I prayed to God, and he answered my prayer."

We moved to Alabama, and Deedra was on a weekly allergy shot, so Norma McClure, a nurse and great Christian friend to my sister Dot, offered to give Deedra her shots. I tried to pay Norma for handling that, but she said, "No, Lane, don't pay me, but whenever you can, just give me a bell." She showed me her collection of gorgeous bells of all sizes.

Mother went into remission after several trips to Birmingham and several radiation treatments, and Frank's injury healed; we moved back to Chattanooga so he could go back to work.

We were hoping Mama would overcome this horrible thing called cancer, but even with treatments, it took her from us. That was so hard. How do you give up the one who had always been there to love and care for you, to help you get through the bad things that life has to offer?

The nuclear plants were finishing being built, so they were laying off the construction workers. Unfortunately, Frank was laid off. The next week, Frank got a call from the carpenters' local in

Houston to help build a nuclear plant in Bay Town, Texas. Bay Town was a small city not far from Houston. We moved from Chattanooga and leased an apartment in Houston. Houston was a great place to live. I went to work at Mervyn's as a sales clerk and was soon promoted to floor manager. Not forgetting the kindness that Norma had shown us, I bought a bell and mailed it to her.

We enjoyed living in Houston, but when the job ended and Frank was laid off, we put our furniture and lots of boxes in storage along with the creepy Spanish picture and went back home to Chattanooga, where we rented a furnished apartment. Frank got several small jobs and was working off and on, and I was working at Sears. Times were hard, and the economy was bad, so it was hard for Frank to find a job. He called other carpenters' locals across the United States and found a job in Phoenix, so we moved there.

Phoenix was a beautiful place—a desert filled with cactus, sand, and palm trees. At night, the sky was not black—it was a beautiful navy blue. The moonrise was amazing; the moon was huge and bright. Frank and I saw our first moonrise there when we were taking a walk. Looking across the desert at what looked like the end of the earth, we saw this big, bright, orange light slowly rising, getting bigger, and covering half the sky.

"What's that, Frank?" I asked.

"I don't know," he answered.

"Oh my goodness!" I said. "The earth is coming to an end! We better run for the mountains."

He laughed. "We don't have any mountains to run to."

It was such a beautiful place with a beauty that was so different from the beautiful mountains in Chattanooga. We were excited about the new city, and Frank went to work right away. However, the job didn't last very long; he was laid off again. It seemed that we just couldn't get ahead no matter what we tried or where we lived. We were talking about what the heck we were going to do so far from home with no money and no job.

Then there was a knock at the door. Frank opened the door, and we could not believe it; there stood Sheila and Misty. Jim Boy had gone to Florida to be with his dad. They had come all the way from Alabama, and there we were—not knowing what we were going to do—stay or leave.

On Monday, Frank and Sheila went out looking for jobs. Deedra was already in school, and Sheila enrolled Misty in school. Sheila got a job in downtown Phoenix in the next few days, and Frank got work before the week was out. I also got a job working at a photography lab on the night shift. *Things aren't going to be so bad after all*, I thought. *We'll make it some way, somehow.*

Soon, school was out for the summer, and Jim's dad put him on a plane to Phoenix. We had our family back; the last piece of the puzzle was then in place.

One day while I was getting ready for work, the doorbell started ringing and didn't stop. It was as if someone was holding it down in anger. I threw on my housecoat and rushed to the door. There stood this strange, dead-looking woman dressed in black. Before I could shut the door, she put her foot inside. I said, "You better move your foot or I'm going to hurt you."

She laughed a silly laugh and in a frightening voice said, "Nooo, I'm going tooo hurttt youuu."

I slammed the door as hard as I could and locked it. I heard her moan in pain. Nervous and shaking, I went to my room to finish dressing for work. I drove to work very upset; I wanted to calm down before I got there, so I pulled in at the first McDonalds I came to and ordered a Pepsi. I sat in a booth and sipped on it till I could find the courage to return to the traffic.

In about a year, Sheila took her kids and headed back to Alabama. It was lonely without them, but if that was what made her happy, we were happy for her.

Frank's work was coming and going; small jobs were all that he was getting. "When I get another job, we're going to save all we can, and when it ends, we're gonna leave here."

"Where will we go?" I asked.

"I don't know," he said. "Just wherever I can find a job."

He got another small job, and we saved every penny we could.

When he got laid off, he started calling the carpenters' locals. We really wanted to get back to Chattanooga, but when he called them, he learned they were not doing anything. He started calling cities going east and said, "We'll choose the first city that has any work for me."

The first city with work was Dallas, so we were Texas bound. The carpenters' local for the Dallas/Fort Worth area was in Arlington, a small city between Dallas and Fort Worth. "This looks good," Frank said. "We'll get a place here."

We got a motel and a newspaper. Frank went to the local, and I searched the paper for an apartment. Frank came back and said he had a job starting the next Monday. We took the rest of the day off and just rested.

We found the right apartment and left for Houston to get our furniture out of storage. We enjoyed opening the boxes of our things we had not seen for a long time. Deedra would open a box and with excitement say, "Look, Mom! I forgot I even had this." I came to the Spanish pictures and took them to the sofa. "Frank, please hang these over the sofa," I said.

"Are you sure you want these where you can see them?" he asked.

"Yeah, it'll be okay," I answered.

Frank hung them, and I noticed the bullfighter was still moving his eyes to watch me, but that time, his eyes looked squinting and evil as though he were the devil himself.

"You may be mad because we had to leave you in storage for so long, but we couldn't help it," I said looking back at him with evil in my eyes also.

We found the right apartment. Deedra was sixteen then. I had to find a school for her. Lamar was the high school for that area, and it was a good school. She got a job working nights and weekends at McDonalds. She met Tommy Strandlie there, and they started dating. Her life was going well for a teenager.

I went to work at Meisel's Photography Lab, so we were all three working. Deedra was a good teenager, and she helped us so much since she had her own money. She bought all her clothes and earned her own spending money. We always felt so blessed to have her; she never gave us the problems that some teenagers gave their parents.

Tom was a good boy too, so we didn't have to worry about him, and she had met several other friends at the pool, one being Joe Vogel. He was a little older but a good friend to all the teenagers; he always reminded them to behave themselves. They respected Joe, so they listened to his advice.

We were not being bothered by strange, scary things and had not even thought about it for a long time, so our life was normal, and we were enjoying every moment.

Tommy graduated first, and Deedra a year later. They attended the prom together, and both were styling and looking so good. They broke up for reasons unknown; they were seeking other companions since they had been the first for each other.

Sheila worked at TVA in Muscle Shoals, Alabama, so she helped Deedra get a job with her. We helped her get a car and get everything ready for the move. We were so sad; our baby was leaving home, but we were happy for her too. We drove behind her all the way to Alabama. She would be living and working with Sheila, who would see that things were good for her. We stayed the weekend at Sheila's. "Spread your little wings and fly," I told Deedra as I hugged her goodbye.

We were quiet on the trip home. It just wasn't the same without our little girl. "We knew this day would come," Frank said.

"I know, but I don't think there is any way to prepare for it," I answered while trying to hide my tears. "She'll always be my baby."

Back at home, we had a lot to get used to; it had been a long time since it was just the two of us. We were doing what we could to be a happy couple—spending the weekends curled up on the sofa, going out for dinner, stopping for a good night of shooting pool, and just enjoying being together.

It had been several years since my mother had passed, and Frank's mother was ninety and in poor health; she was not doing well. His brothers and sisters decided it would be better to sell her house and take care of her in their homes.

We visited her in Alabama at Stella's house. Stella went into the bedroom and came out with an antique picture of her grandmother in an antique frame. "Will you take this picture home with you and make copies of it?" she asked.

"Yes I will," I answered. "How many do you need?"

"About seven should be enough," she said. "I just want enough to give all my kids one picture of their great-great-grandmother. Frank can have this original, and you can mail me the copies."

The woman in the picture was very stern looking, very prim and proper; in fact, she looked like she would have been a hateful, mean, and controlling person. She was dressed in a very good dress of the times with the stand-up collar and lace.

"Did you ever know your great-grandmother?" I asked Frank.

"No" he answered, "and by the look on her face, it may have been a good thing."

At home, I put the picture in the living room chair so I would be sure to take it to work the next morning.

We were lying in bed when we started hearing moaning and groaning in the living room. We got out of bed; Frank switched the light on and started for the living room with me right behind him. There was nothing there, but the picture had tumbled over and was lying face down in the chair.

We made sure the doors and windows were locked; we checked every closet and every room in the apartment before we went back to bed. "You don't think that was the picture making those strange sounds, do you, Frank?" I asked.

"I don't know," he said, "but let's hope not."

We were tired from the long trip, and we fell asleep with me on his arm and as close as I could get.

At work, I copied, printed, and made a couple of extra prints of the picture in case the seven weren't enough. I put the prints in the mail and returned the original to its antique frame; I put it in a closet.

I was cleaning the apartment one weekend and went into Deedra's room to clean it. Seeing her room was a sad experience. She had left some of her special possessions such as her ventriloquist doll, "Emmett Kelly the hobo clown", her blanket, the pictures she had taken with her friends, and a lot of her clothes. My baby was gone; the nest was empty.

I said, "We don't really need Deedra's bedroom anymore, Frank, so why don't we start looking for a one-bedroom?"

"Sounds good to me," he said, "and cheaper too."

It didn't take long before we found just the right apartment in Fort Worth. It was a cute apartment, just the right size for us—one bedroom and one bath meant less to clean. As I was putting things away, I sat the antique picture on the dresser in our bedroom until

I could find that special place for it. I also put the hobo clown on the dresser. Deedra had played with it so much that the pull string had come loose from its slot. It had been sitting in the closet for a long time; I thought we might be able to have it fixed for her.

That night was good, and when the alarm clock went off, Frank slipped out of bed and went to work without waking me. I was awakened by groaning and moaning. I opened my eyes and I was startled at what I saw—the grandma picture. The arms were reaching out of the picture at me. I jumped out of the bed and started trembling all over. Not knowing what else to do, I threw a pillow at the picture, and it turned over on the dresser.

After the picture fell, the doll started moving its arms and mouth as if someone was pulling the string. I went to the living room to try to calm down, but the Spanish bullfighter was watching me too. All I could think about was how that picture was reaching for me and the doll was trying so hard to talk. I started thinking of how Frank's mother had never liked me, so maybe her grandmother was trying to harm me as a gift for her granddaughter.

That evening after Frank came home from work, I was telling him about the picture when the phone rang; Lloyd, Frank's brother, told us their mother had passed away.

We packed and headed for Alabama, a twelve-hour trip. The funeral was nice; arrangements had been made by her five sons and daughters who lived there. We stayed only long enough for the funeral.

After we left, Frank said, "Maybe the picture was trying to warn us that Mother was dying."

"That could have been the reason," I said, "but it sure wrecked my nerves for the rest of the day, and it doesn't explain the doll."

"What doll?" he asked.

"After I threw the pillow and knocked the picture over, the doll started moving its arms and mouth as though someone was pulling its string."

It was late at night when we got home, and we were so tired. At least we had a few hours left before we had to go to work. As soon as we entered the apartment, Frank went straight to the bedroom, got the picture of his great-grandmother and Emmitt the doll, took them outside, and threw them in the dumpster. We got in the bed and fell asleep after we had our goodnight kiss.

CHAPTER 7
An Abusive Visitor

The next day, we needed to do the laundry, so I got it ready, and we carried the baskets downstairs to the laundry room hoping there were some washers available. The baskets were heavy, so thank goodness it was close by. As soon as we went through the door, I realized we had forgotten the dryer sheets. "Oh heck, Frank," I said, "we don't have the dryer sheets. I'll run back and get them while you put the clothes in the washers."

"Okay," Frank said, "just so you hurry back."

"I'll be back before you even have time to miss me," I said with a laugh.

A storm seemed to be coming up; the sky was rolling with dark clouds, and some lightning was going on. I made my way up the stairs and entered the apartment. I reached for the light switch and flicked it on. Something seemed eerie, but I couldn't see anything out of the ordinary, so I started to the linen closet for the dryer sheets. Something that I could not see grabbed me and roughly shoved me down on the sofa in a sitting position. I was stunned and scared. I didn't know what was happening. I started trying to get up but could not move. Something was holding my feet to the floor and my body to the sofa. I was so scared that I was crying, shaking, and screaming for help hoping the neighbor next door would hear me. This strange force was hitting me; I felt the pain, but I couldn't see a thing. I kept screaming and trying to get up, but getting up wasn't going to happen unless whatever was holding me down decided to let me go. "Help! Please help me!" I yelled as tears were streaming down my face.

Finally, the door opened—there was Frank. "So you forgot to come back," he said with a smile.

"Help me, Frank!" I said through my tears.

"What's going on?"

"Help me, Frank. I can't get up. Something's holding me down and has been hitting me."

Frank took my hands and started pulling; he realized I wasn't joking—I really could not get up and he couldn't pull me up. Something was holding me down, something stronger than he was.

"What on earth is this?" he asked.

Still shaking and crying, I felt the release of whatever was holding me, so I stood up. I was so relieved that it was over. I fell into Frank's arms. He held me tight for a while before we went back to the laundry room. We got the laundry done and returned to the apartment. I put the laundry away while Frank sat on the sofa and was getting ready to watch TV.

"I'm getting in the shower, Frank," I yelled from the bathroom. I started taking my clothes off and noticed all the red places on my legs and arms. "Frank, come see what that unknown force did to me."

Frank came in the bathroom and couldn't believe what he saw. "This is bad, Lane," he said. "Whatever that was wanted to hurt you."

"It did hurt me, Frank," I said.

I got in the shower, and Frank went back to watch TV. After all the drama I had been through, the shower was relaxing. I took my time enjoying the warm water. I got out, dried off, wrapped the towel around me, and started for the bedroom to put my pajamas on when suddenly there in the hallway I bumped into a transparent figure of a tall man, a cruel-looking man, but it felt like a person, a real flesh-and-blood person. I yelled, and Frank came running. "What's going on now?" he asked.

I was so stunned that I could barely speak. "I don't know, Frank. I've never felt anything like this. It was a transparent man, a mean-looking man. I bumped into him, and he felt like a real person, but I could see through him."

We sat on the sofa; Frank held my hand until I calmed down. It seemed I was crying and shaking for a long time. "The man is what was holding me and hitting me, Frank. I hate that I was born with a veil," I said through the sobbing.

"I know you do, honey," Frank said, "and I hate seeing you have to go through this. It just doesn't seem right. If I could make it all go away, I would in a heartbeat."

I went to the bedroom to get out of the towel and got dressed for bed. I turned to start for the living room, and there it was leaning against the door frame and looking even meaner than before. Screaming for Frank, I sat on the bed and covered my face with my hands and prepared for the worst. I heard Frank rushing to help me.

"What is it, Lane?"

"It's that same mean-looking man," I said. I removed my hands from my face and looked toward the door; the transparent devil was gone. I fell over on Frank, and he held me as I cried. We prayed together and finished the night watching an old episode of *Gunsmoke* in which Marshall Dillon went upstairs to visit with Miss Kitty.

I calmed down, and we went to bed. We were so exhausted from the trip, going to work with only a few hours' sleep, and getting the laundry done that we fell asleep as soon as our heads hit the pillows.

We went to work the next day letting the bad things that had taken place disappear from our lives; other things like making a living had to be the top priority.

CHAPTER 8

A Pleasant Surprise, A Good Move, A Tragic Event

In Alabama, Deedra met Jason Roberts. We learned they were in a relationship and she was going to have our grandbaby. We had never met Jason, but we would be going to Sheffield when the baby was born; I hoped we could get to know him then.

A few months later, we got the call—Deedra was in labor and at the hospital, so we left for Alabama. She gave birth to Tyler Lee Roberts, a gorgeous boy for us to love. Oh, how we hated to leave him and Deedra; it was like leaving a big part of us. We said goodbye with kisses and hugs. Jason seemed like a good guy; we hoped they were mature enough to do everything right.

We were working so much that it was hard to even consider going for a visit, so we talked about moving back to our hometown just to be with our daughter and little Tyler as soon as Frank's job ended.

Tyler was about ten months old when the day came that we moved to Alabama. We were happy about the move. We found a nice place on Colbert Heights Mountain in Tuscumbia. As we were unloading the U-Haul truck, I noticed the Spanish pictures and picked up the beautiful dancing lady. Underneath that one, the evil eyes of the bullfighter were staring at me and turning to the side to watch me as I was walking away. After taking the dancer in the apartment, I went back for the bullfighter. He was looking at me with the most glaring, hateful look I had ever seen. I looked back at it and said, "I'm thinking of getting rid of you so you'll never look at me and others with your demon eyes again." The picture started shaking and moving, and it fell off the tall box it was sitting on. With it still jumping around, I yelled for Frank, and he came running. "What is it, Lane?" he asked and then he noticed. "Oh, I see. It's the picture. I'm getting rid of it." The picture became still, and Frank carried it in the apartment.

When Frank started his next job, he took both Spanish pictures to work and gave them to another worker. Later, when Frank asked him how the pictures were working out, he said his wife loved them hanging over her sofa.

I started babysitting for Deedra while she worked. That was what life was all about—just being with my little dude all day every day and watching him grow, helping him learn to talk, and especially teaching him to play Nintendo and watching him jump and take a step every time Mario did. I was doing what grandmas do best—spoiling their grandchildren.

One evening, my cousin Bud Newman called and asked, "Has anyone called you, Lane?"

I could tell by his voice that he was about to say something bad. "If it's bad news, Bud, please don't tell me. I'll let you talk to Frank," I said.

"Okay, then let me speak to Frank," he said.

I just knew this was something horrible, something I didn't want to hear. I handed Frank the phone and went to the bedroom. I lay down on the bed and covered my face with my hands.

Frank entered the room and lay down beside me and said, "You have to hear this, Lane. It's not gonna go away, and it's gonna be hard, so prepare yourself."

I was already crying; the day my daddy died was flashing through my mind. Frank put his arm around me and said, "I hate to tell you this, but it's Brenda." I threw my hands over my ears not wanting to hear the rest. He paused then said, "She's dead."

I jumped up screaming, "No! This can't be! It just can't be."

"It's true," Frank said. "Sheila went to Brenda's and found her in the bathtub."

Brenda had made her own funeral arrangements, so we didn't

have any of that to do. We just had to clean out her apartment. I was going to miss my sister so badly. I had loved her so much and for so long.

It was hard trying to get over the death of my sister, the one I had grown up with and depended on for everything, the one who had been my best friend. We had been through so much together as children and had made so many pacts, even one pact where we did it Indian style and really cut our fingers with a razor blade. She had placed her bleeding finger on top of mine letting our blood run together as we made promises to always be there for each other.

About a week later, after Frank and Tyler had gone to bed, I was sitting on the sofa sketching some cartoon art and was startled by a gentle nudge. I looked up thinking I was going to see Frank or Tyler, but instead, there was Brenda. She was kneeling on the floor in front of me with one hand on my arm. She took my hand and with her soft voice said, "It's gonna be all right, Aline. It's gonna be all right." She gently kissed my hand and then she was gone. It had been a long time since I had heard that name and heard her say, "It's gonna be all right, Aline." Then she slowly faded away "I love you, Brenda. I love you and will forever," I said hoping she could hear me.

CHAPTER 9
Retirement Years

We moved to a place on the Tennessee River thinking this would be great for us when Frank retired. There was a deck out back where we could sit and watch the boaters, and we also had a pier over the water where Frank could fish.

Frank decided he would work one more job and that would be his last. He was called to go on a job in Atlanta, which meant he would be gone all week and come home only on weekends. I didn't want to go to Atlanta, so he left with some other carpenters from the Shoals area. I tried to make the best of the lonely nights while he was gone doing things such as helping my cousin, Bud, paint his apartment, visiting my sisters, and taking my evening walks at Walmart.

I was beginning to not like living on the water. Lizards would get in the house. "I don't like lizards," I told Frank, "and it's so far from town. I just can't get used to that. You know I've always been a city girl."

"I know, Lane, so we'll see about finding another place," he said.

Frank left again for another week. I had nothing to do one day, so I thought I would just take a hot bath and go visit with Sheila. The house was laid out such that when you entered the bathroom, the washer and dryer area was first and then the bath area, both being in the same room. I filled the tub with warm water; I bathed lying there just thinking about how much I was missing Frank. I thought I would stay in the tub a little longer than usual, but I heard something scooting across the floor. I got out, dried off, and put on my gown and bathrobe. I started for the door and what I saw made my heart skip a beat. What was I going to do being there all alone? Something or someone had moved the washer in front of the door. I was thinking I would not be strong enough to move the heavy washer, and the only window in the room was up too high for me to reach.

I went to the washer, and with strength I didn't realize I had, I moved it back to its original place and opened the door. Water was flooding the floor coming from the connection pipe. I turned the faucet off.

I heard strange sounds coming from the living room. When I got there, I saw the door swinging back and forth rapidly, but I couldn't see anyone. I went to the bedroom, put on my jeans and a shirt, picked up the pistol, and returned to the living room and the swinging door. I pointed the gun at the door and commanded it to stop. "If you don't stop, I'll shoot," I said, and to my surprise, the door stopped swinging. I grabbed a change of clothes, my necessary things, my purse and keys, and ran out the door saying, "Whoever you are, you can have this house," and I left.

I stayed at the Day's Inn that night, and the next day I took Sheila and Bud with me back to the house. Deedra's friend, Joe Vogel, being a Catholic, had mailed us a bottle of holy water from Texas. I went to the kitchen and took the bottle from the drawer. I really didn't know how to do this, but I threw the holy water, made the sign of the cross, and said, "Leave this house in Jesus's name! Leave this house in Jesus's name!" I went through the house doing this in each room.

That night, I returned to the motel and called Frank to tell him what had happened. I told him I wanted to move, and I knew of an apartment that was empty just two doors down from Sheila.

"Okay," Frank said. "If that's what you want, we'll move this weekend."

I stayed at the motel for a week. By the time Frank came back, I had the apartment leased, so we moved in.

The first thing I did was use the holy water throughout the apartment not knowing if it would really help or not; however, from then on, the holy water stayed in the living room on the end table.

When Tyler was seven, he was staying a while with Poppa and me. We had fun playing X-box games with him. Frank and I enjoyed sitting in the gorgeous flower garden watching the sunset, seeing the evening star and moon appear, and sitting there until all the stars came out.

One night while we were sitting in the garden, Tyler laid down his game controller and came outside where we were. He looked at me a little strangely and asked, "Memaw, how could this be? I just saw you in the kitchen, then walking down the hall, and going into the bedroom."

"I don't know baby," I answered. "I've been sitting out here."

That night, after Frank and Tyler went to bed, I saw the back of a woman dressed in a long white gown that was flowing as she was going down the hallway toward the bedroom. I was so scared, but not wanting to wake Tyler and Frank, I grabbed the holy water and rushed to this woman before she could go into the room where Tyler and Frank were sleeping. When I got to her, I threw the water in the sign of the cross and said, "Leave this house in Jesus's name."

Immediately, she started making moaning sounds as though the water was painful. She slowly faded away. Not wanting Tyler to be scared, I kept that to myself until Frank and I could be alone.

Deedra's and Jason's relationship had fell apart and Deedra had been dating Joe Vogel. She moved back to Texas and married Joe. We had to say goodbye to our precious grandson.

Joe was a good husband for Deedra and the very best dad for Tyler. Tyler respected Joe and proudly told me what a great dad he was. Tyler and Deedra were happy, and if there had been such a thing as a son-in-law catalog, we would have ordered Joe Vogel; he was just that precious.

Frank retired, so we were planning a trip. We chose Route 66. We had been on lots of trips during our life together, but this one was going to be the best, the most exciting one because we were no longer working and we would not have to rush.

One Sunday after church for reasons I didn't know, I said to Frank, "We need to go to Dot's."

"Why do we need to go to Dot's?" he asked.

"There's a dog that her neighbor has, and I'm going to get that dog," I said.

"What makes you think that woman will give you her dog?" Frank asked.

"I don't know," I answered. "It's just that something is telling me to get that dog."

We got to Dot's in Muscle Shoals, and she stepped out on her deck and asked us to come in.

"No," I said. "I've come to get that dog your neighbor has, the one you've been telling me about, the one that's kept in the pen." She looked at me funny and asked, "How do you know she'll give you her dog?"

"I don't know how I know, I just know," I answered.

Dot walked with me to her neighbor's house. I stopped at the pen and saw this gorgeous little black cocker spaniel looking at me through the wire fence. "I've come to take you home with me," I said to the dog while Dot knocked on the woman's door. Dot asked her if she would give me her dog, and the woman said, "No, she can't have my dog."

I left the pen, and so did the dog through the gate that was partly open. We went up to the woman. The little dog sat down beside her owner's feet and looked as if she were listening to every word. Dot said to me, "You and Frank are about to go on the Route 66 trip, so what would you do with the dog?"

"We'd take her with us," I said.

The woman said, "Okay, you can have her. She loves to ride."

The little dog ran back into the pen, and I was thinking she didn't want to go, but she came out with her only toy in her mouth and stood there beside me as I put her leash on. We headed back to Dot's. This little dog was so ready to go, and she never looked back. Her name was on her birth certificate—Midnight Satin Rockette. She went straight to Frank, and from that moment on, she was Frank's baby, and he called her Ol' Rock. We loved this little cocker spaniel, and she loved us, but Frank was her dad and I was the one who fed them. We learned later from her original owner that she was a show dog and had won a blue ribbon. I felt that little Rockette was a blessing for Frank and me.

We went on the Route 66 trip and saw lots of beautiful things—the Petrified Forest, the Grand Canyon, rocks as big as a house, rocks that looked as if God had started to create them, stopped, and said, "This is good enough."

We saw a sign reading Drive-Thru Animal Zoo. "Let's stop here," Frank said. "Ol' Rock will like this." Rockette loved the zoo with big animals poking their heads through the window to get treats Frank purchased at the ticket window. We had a wonderful time. We stopped in Texas on the way home and spent some time with Joe, Deedra, and Tyler.

We bought a house in Sheffield that needed to be restored and updated. I said, "Frank, we'll have fun doing the work ourselves."

"Oh yeah, right," he said.

"We can try, and if we don't like it, we can get workers in to do it for us, okay?" I asked.

"Yeah, we can do that," he answered.

Within two weeks, we had signed the papers and were moving in.

We started the work right away doing things like putting in new cabinets, putting in the washer and dryer, and getting the heat and air conditioning installed. We put in tile in the kitchen and carpet in the living room and hallway, but we kept the hardwood floors in the bedrooms; we sanded and stained them.

Every day when we got up, we would find two different colored marbles on the new floors even though we didn't have marbles.

Then the painting started. We painted each room a different color, and the guest bedroom became a big problem. "Frank, come look!" I yelled.

He came from the kitchen and asked, "What's up?" but then he noticed the bedroom that had been beige the night before but was then the same blue it had been before we painted it. "Oh my gosh!" he said. "How could this happen?"

"I don't know, but I don't like it. I liked the beige," I said. Looking on the floor, I saw two more marbles. We tried painting it again and again, but each time, it would be back blue in the morning and the marbles would return.

Frank and I went across the street and talked with the neighbor, an elderly man, about who the previous owners were. Frank asked, "Did you know who lived here before us?"

He answered, "Yes, I knew them well. They were an older couple, and they lived there until the man became sick and passed away."

Frank asked, "Did he die in the house?"

The neighbor answered, "Oh no. He died at the hospital."

Frank visited with this man several times and learned that the man's bedroom was blue and that the man collected marbles. The room stayed blue, and the marbles kept coming in all colors and sizes.

After only seven months, we finished the remodeling and put the house up for sale. It sold in two weeks. We spread the marbles in the flower garden and around the shrubs.

We moved to Florence and were visiting different congregations all over the Shoals area trying to find one where we would be happy. When we visited the Florence Boulevard Church of Christ, the first person who came to welcome us was an elderly gentleman who put his hand out to shake hands and introduced himself: "I'm Gilbert Kretzer. I want to welcome you to Florence Boulevard." My mouth fell open; there I was over sixty, and this was the preacher who had been at Valdosta when I was little. I was so happy; I knew we had found just the right place to worship our God.

Frank kept coughing a lot, so when his carpenters' local mailed him a notice that the asbestos doctor was going to be in Decatur, Alabama, he took advantage of the free examination by an expert in the disease. He had been examined by experts two other times and was found to be okay. That time, however, he was diagnosed as having asbestosis. This was a sad time in our life. We had to make many changes, and he had to have just the right lung doctor to care for him. He chose Dr. Lynn Randall in Sheffield, whom

Frank decided was the best pulmonary doctor that the Shoals had to offer.

Dr. Randall did a great job treating him for about five years, but on one of Frank's exams and after being x-rayed, Dr. Randall entered the examination room with a different look on his face. "I have bad news, Franklin," he said.

"Let's hear it," Frank said.

"I hate to tell you this, but your x-ray shows you have cancer in your right lung."

Tears started creeping down my face as I reached to hug Frank. Frank looked up at me wanting to be the brave man he had always been and said, "Oh, Lane, I'm okay."

Then came all the radiation treatments. Frank made it fine through them and even said, "This ain't so bad. I feel fine."

When he finished the amount of treatments allowed, he had to have a full-body scan to see what had been accomplished. During our next trip to the Bethesda cancer center, Dr. Stanley Carver came in the room and told Frank that the cancer in the right lung was gone but that his left lung had four tumors. Frank smiled and said, "Well, let's just start radiation on the left one." Dr. Carver said, "I wish we could, but one time is all the radiation you can have. You'll have to have chemotherapy."

Frank started chemotherapy treatments at the North Alabama Cancer Center under Dr. Hermant Posey. Chemo was horrible.

Frank would be so sick that he couldn't get out of bed for at least four days after a treatment, and just about the time he would feel like getting up, it would be time for another treatment. That was not like my Frank, the man who had always been so strong, the one who could do anything, the one who had fought and won so many trials in our married life. I had to hide my daily tears, so I did a lot of my cartoon pencil art to give my attention to something other than the ugly word *cancer*.

The time came. Frank said, "It's time. I need to go to the hospital."

With the emergency lights blinking I drove faster than what was safe to the Helen Keller Hospital in Tuscumbia. Just as the nurse got Frank to the bed in the emergency room, he fell down on the bed. The nurse yelled for the doctor, who came running. The doctor said that Frank was dead. He asked me if I wanted him to try to revive him. I said, "Yes! Please do whatever you can."

He asked me to leave the room and started working on Frank after telling me to call my family in. I was so shocked that I said, "I don't have anyone." I sat down in a chair that a nurse placed by the door for me. My phone rang. It was Sheila; at that moment, I came to my senses and realized I did have someone. Sheila rushed to the hospital, and I called Frank's brother, Lloyd.

In just a few minutes, Sam and Lloyd, both of Frank's brothers, were coming through the ER door; I was not so alone. Deedra, Joe, and Tyler were getting a plane and would be at the hospital in a few hours.

Frank was put in ICU with a tube down his throat; the tube was connected to a machine to breathe for him.

The room was full with everyone there except Jim Boy, who was still in Idaho. Frank didn't open his eyes, but when I took his hand, the words "My Father in heaven" came out of my mouth. I realized it really wasn't me saying that, but I noticed Sam had already bowed his head and Frank was squeezing my hand, so I closed my eyes and finished the prayer.

Misty had left the hospital for the night and was rushing trying to get back from Hackleburg, Alabama. Deedra, Joe, and Tyler were at the motel. Frank passed away. That was the most devastating time of my life. How was I going to get by without Frank? He had been my rock, the one who had made all the major decisions, and he had been my strength for fifty years.

There was the funeral with military honors and a twenty-one-gun salute, and little Rockette was there with her white bows. "Jesus will take care of me," I whispered to Frank as I kissed him for the last time. The casket was closed.

The next years were not easy. I had to take one step at a time trying to do for myself what Frank had always done. I had to make decisions I had never made without Frank. My love was not there. He was gone, and he had taken my heart with him. I didn't know if I could ever be the same loving and smiling person I had always been.

CHAPTER 10

So Few of Us Left

My family is now so broken. Little Rockette passed away. Tyler and Devi live in Texas. Sheila, Jeff, Misty, and Andy live in Tennessee. Jim and JeriLynn with their family are in Idaho. Dot passed away with cancer leaving Curtis alone, although his children, Denise and Chris, visit him often. Joe passed away. And Deedra moved here to be close to me.

A couple of years later, Deedra married Fred Terrell, the most wonderful man in the entire Shoals area. *There are not many of us left here*, I thought. I felt so helpless at times, and even after five years without Frank, it was still so hard. I try so hard to keep smiling; I feel so alone.

At my age, my health is not very good. I went to bed thinking about the family I no longer had and about how blessed we were to have our little Rockette, the little dog I believe was a blessing, the one we never would have had in our life if I had not received a premonition that Frank and I needed this little dog.

I was sad. I fell asleep with tears running down my face. I heard a noise—the sound of a kiss—and I felt something warm on my lips. I opened my eyes and saw Frank leaning over me. He rose, so I got out of the bed. He was dressed in a beautiful white robe, the kind they may have worn in biblical times. He was smiling and slowly fading away. I started crying. "Frank! Please don't go! Please come back!"

For the first time in my life, I was happy that I had been born with a veil.

Ruby Aline "Lane" Baker

Sheila Johnson

CHAPTER 11
Second Chances

by Sheila Johnson, Lane's Younger Sister

Being Lane's younger sister and with the family I had, I grew up with an open mind to things that I did not understand. I had heard the story about my mother's grandfather seeing his wife after she died and had decided he was going with her. He refused to eat another bite, and he died of starvation in a couple of weeks.

I loved listening to my aunt Ruby tell of her experiences. She had seen and heard many things that others had not. She once lived in a haunted house in Arkansas. She told me of a little girl who would swing underneath a big oak tree and sing the prettiest song. She also told me about the floor in an upstairs bedroom that had blood on it. She would scrub that floor on her hands and knees, but the blood would be back the next day.

Two of her brothers came down from Cleveland and replaced the whole floor and told Aunt Ruby, "That stuff won't come back now. We made sure of that." They even slept in that bedroom that night. When they woke up the next morning, the blood was there. Her brothers didn't waste any time heading back to Cleveland.

Having lived with Lane many times through the years, I was used to lights turning on or off for no apparent reason and strange noises that had no explanation.

When I was eighteen, I was expecting my first baby; I left my husband because of his terrible jealousy and moved in with Lane and Frank.

A few days before Christmas, I went into hard labor that lasted fourteen hours. I gave birth to a beautiful baby girl I named Misty Marie. I was so weak that I fell into a deep sleep. It was getting late, so my family and friends had left the hospital assuming that I would feel better in the morning.

I felt myself floating up to the ceiling fully awake. I looked down and saw my body on the bed. I saw a nurse come in to check my vital signs. The nurse turned and hurried out the door. She returned quickly with Dr. Bentley, who started slapping me and with anxiety in his voice saying, "Sheila! Sheila!" He told the nurse, "Keep checking her vitals."

I saw a beautiful light above me, and I started floating through the light. At the end of the light, I saw Red, my stepfather. I was so excited! I said, "Red, I love you, and I've missed you so much."

He said, "Sheila, I love you too, but you can't come here. It's not your time yet. You have to go back."

I started crying. I said, "Red, I just had a beautiful baby girl, and I want you to meet her."

He said, "If I can, I'll come to meet your baby soon, but go back, Sheila."

The next thing I knew, I was telling Dr. Bentley to stop slapping me. I heard him tell the nurse to be sure and monitor me closely through the night. When Lane told me about the shadow she had seen leaning over Misty's crib, I knew that that just had to have been Red giving my baby a kiss.

After Misty was born, I got a divorce, got a job, and started college; Mom watched Misty for me. Lane, Frank, and baby Deedra were moving to Chattanooga, and they helped me get an apartment in Sheffield before they left. I missed them so badly. I felt that I had been with them all my life, and then they were so far away. Misty and I visited them as often as possible.

They had very strange noises happening in their home that anyone could hear—a newborn crying, someone walking hurriedly from Deedra's bedroom to the other end of the trailer, and scary noises coming out of their stereo. I was familiar with the strange things and noises; it seemed that Lane attracted these happenings.

I would tell Mother about the strange things, and she would say that she didn't believe in ghosts and that strange things happened because Lane had been born with a veil.

One time, Mother went with Misty and me to visit Lane. She was sitting on the sofa when we heard a baby crying and someone running through the trailer. She looked at me and asked, "Where are the girls?"

I said, "They're outside on the swing set, Mom."

We had to cut our visit short and head back to Tuscumbia. When we got in the car, Mother said, "I don't want to talk about it. I've heard things all my life, and I don't want to talk about it."

I put a Roy Clark cassette in the tape player, and she was happy. She said, "Roy makes you want to stop the car and go juking in the middle of the road." I just laughed.

I was close to graduating from college when I met and fell in love with Jimmy Daily. We got married, and I was expecting my second baby. I told him I wanted to move to Chattanooga and find a good job. He agreed to the move.

I finished college, had my baby boy I named James Delaneo Daily—James after his dad and Delaneo after Frank, whom I thought so much of. I called him Jim.

My children and I moved to Chattanooga and stayed with Lane and Frank until I could find a job and move out. I got a job in just a few days at the public library and became friends for life with Debra, a sweet woman who was my age. I moved out to a mobile home in Ooltewah just about a mile from Lane. Jimmy moved to Ooltewah and got a construction job in Chattanooga.

He was a loving father to Jim and Misty. Jimmy was doing really well for a few months until he found a pool hall in downtown Chattanooga. He was pretty good at shooting pool and loved it. He started staying out until late at night and started gambling his money away.

One night, he came home without his new boots. "Jimmy, where are your boots?" I asked.

"I lost them shooting pool," he answered. "They were my boots. Why do I have to explain it to you?"

"I'm sorry, Jimmy, but this just isn't going to work," I said.

I started having stomach pains that were so bad that I saw my gynecologist. He ran some tests and told me that I had cervical cancer in second stage and that I needed a hysterectomy, but I told him I couldn't afford to be off the eight weeks that were required at that time because I had two little ones who were counting on me. He told me that they could try taking out the part where the cancer was and see if that would work. I opted for that.

Later that evening, I told Jimmy about my cancer and asked him if he would go through it with me. He said, "No, I don't believe you have cancer."

I said, "Then you need to get out."

He moved back to the Shoals area, and I got Lane to take me in for surgery. Thank goodness for sisters.

When I went back to my doctor, he told me they couldn't get it all. That was the beginning of a lot of smaller surgeries taking a piece out at a time and burning and freezing cancer cells that kept popping up.

After a couple of years, I was ready to move back to Tuscumbia, so the kids and I packed up and moved back home with Mother.

I applied for a job at TVA and got it. I had to travel to each nuclear plant and do surveys. I would leave on Monday mornings and return Friday afternoons. Sometimes, I would call Mom crying and saying, "I miss you and the kids so much."

"We're doing fine, Sheila. Just get your job done," she would say.

I would talk to the kids for a few minutes and let them know I would be home Friday.

After a few years of survey work, I was transferred to the construction services branch as a secretary. At least I got to come home every evening.

Mother started getting a bad cough that didn't go away. She kept saying it was just the flu. After about two months, she finally went to the doctor, who told her she had lung cancer. She had radiation treatments and chemotherapy, and she was in remission for a while, but the cancer came back worse than before.

She was admitted in the hospital in November right after my twenty-eighth birthday. My sisters and I took turns sitting with her. On the twenty-first, a Sunday, I went in to relieve Dot and Lane. Just as they were walking out the door, I asked Dot, "Please give me a cigarette."

"No, you quit smoking," she said.

I said, "I don't want to smoke it. I just want to chew on it." She gave me one.

I heard Mom talking to me, but she wasn't able to speak. She kept telling me to read a story to her. I picked up a *True Story* magazine that was lying there. I looked at the names of the stories in the magazine, and something told me to read a particular story, which turned out to be a story about a mother and her adult daughter; the mother had gotten sick just before the holidays. I threw the magazine down and walked over to the window. It was a pretty day outside; I thought if a person had to die, I guess the Lord's Day would be a good day.

Mother grunted, "Uh-huh."

I went to her side and held her hand. I asked, "Mom, are you hearing me?"

She squeezed my hand. In my head, I heard her say, *Finish the story.* I picked up the magazine and read about the daughter losing her mother. The mother told her daughter to be strong and carry on for her children. The story made me cry.

The nurse came in and told me to call the family in. I made that dreaded phone call and sat down staring at Mom. I heard her say that her mother was there and that she was going with her, that she would be okay. I looked at the two nurses who had entered the room thinking that surely they had heard my mom. One of the nurses said, "She's gone now."

I said, "No. Didn't you just hear her?"

One nurse said, "Honey, she didn't say anything. She's passed away."

I was so scared and nervous. Two of my cousins stepped into the room to visit. They realized Mom had passed away, so they stayed with me until my sisters got there.

I did a lot of crying over the next few days. The night after the funeral, I dreamed I was walking by a telephone booth at the bottom of some very wide stairs; the phone started ringing. I answered it, and it was my mother. She said, "Sheila, I just wanted you to know that I'm okay. I want you to carry on with your life and take good care of Misty and Jim."

I looked up at the top of the stairs and saw her standing there in a long white robe. I started screaming, "Wait for me, Mom!"

She said, "You can't come yet, Sheila. I love you, but you can't come. You have things you have to do."

I dropped the phone. As I started to step on the stairs, they disappeared. I woke up crying hysterically. I felt that my mom had given me a wonderful gift and the inspiration to carry on.

Years went by, and I lost my playmate, my best friend ever, my nephew Clay, due to a massive heart attack. My sister Dot told me that he had visited them and told them it was going to be old Sheila's birthday next month and he was going to give me a call and tell me I was older than him at that point. We called each other every birthday. I was five months older than him, so when it was his birthday, I would call him and let him know he wasn't younger than me, and when it was my birthday, he would call and let me know I was older than him.

My heart was broken when they called me and said he had had a heart attack and was at the hospital. I jumped in the car and headed to the hospital. When I got there, they said he had passed. I was devastated. I cried for days.

About a week after he died, I was in bed and felt something tickling my toes. I kicked, and it stopped. After a moment, the tickling started again. I kicked again, and it stopped. The third time the tickling started, I kicked Ricky, the one I had been with for thirteen years, and I kicked him hard. He woke up and asked, "What?"

I said, "Quit tickling my toes."

He said, "I'm not tickling your toes," and he went back to sleep.

I lay back down and was wondering if I had been imagining things when the tickling started again. I sat up, and there was Clay with a big smile on his face. He floated to my side of the bed and held out his hand to me. I took his hand and said, "Clay, I can't go with you yet. Are you okay? I love you, Clay."

He never said anything; he just kept smiling. When he started fading away, I begged him, "Please don't go, Clay. Please come back." He let go of my hand and was gone.

Ricky sat up and asked, "Who are you talking to?"

"It was Clay, Ricky," I answered. I started crying. Ricky held me close until I could calm down.

On my birthday, the phone rang, and I answered. There was a lot of static, but I heard Clay saying, "Happy birthday," and then no sound, no static. Every few years on my birthday, I'd get a phone call with a lot of static, and though I never heard a voice, I knew in my heart it was Clay, and I would tell him I loved him.

Ricky passed away from diabetes, and I became disabled with the same disease. I lost my job, my car, and my home. I moved to Idaho to stay with my son Jim and his family until I could get my disability started.

Jimmy, my ex-husband and Jim's dad, had passed away a few years earlier. Jim and his wife, JeriLynn, took care of Jimmy the last few years of his life. He had been a good grandfather to their two daughters and their son, Delano.

One day, they were going to the store when Delano was three. As they pulled out of the driveway, Delano started screaming from the back seat, "There's Pawpaw! He's come back! He's waving at me." That startled Jim and JeriLynn, so Jim told her some of the things that had happened in our family.

The next incident occurred a few days later. Delano was sitting at the kitchen table talking with someone and laughing. Jim and JeriLynn assumed he was talking to an imaginary friend until Delano said, "Pawpaw, please don't go."

Jim asked Delano, "Have you been talking to Pawpaw?"

Delano nodded.

"What did Pawpaw say?" JeriLynn asked.

Delano said, "Pawpaw told me he had to leave. He said he would always love me and to eat all the cookies."

Delano hasn't seen him since that time.

After I moved back to Alabama, I stayed with Lane while I was looking for a place to rent since I had started receiving my disability. My daughter, Misty, decided to move closer to her job and told me we could be roommates. That sounded good especially since her job was right around the corner, so if I needed her, she could be there in a minute. I enjoyed living there. Misty had a little dog named Miracle. He was my buddy. He loved sitting on the porch with me watching the traffic go by, and he loved going for walks every day.

One day, I wasn't feeling well, so I stayed in bed. I heard Miracle growling in the living room, so I got up and went to see what he was growling at. He sat there looking up as though he were looking at someone. Every time I got up to check on him, he would growl a vicious growl with his teeth showing as if he were about to attack someone that was behind me.

I checked the entire apartment but saw nothing. I checked to be sure the doors were locked. I told Miracle, "There's nothing here, boy." He just kept sitting in the same spot. I went back to bed and lay down. I started hearing music that sounded like it was from an earlier time than my lifetime. Miracle was still in the other room growling. All of a sudden, he ran and jumped on my bed. He was shaking and barking ferociously at the hallway. I looked at the hallway and saw a man dressed in black with a hat on. That man went in Misty's room even though her door was closed. I held Miracle and said, "You know we have to go check."

I put Miracle down and grabbed my baseball bat out of the closet. I started to Misty's room with Miracle right at my heels. When I reached for the doorknob, Miracle started growling again. I threw the door open holding my bat ready to attack someone or something, but I saw nothing. I told Miracle, "Okay, we need to check under the bed and in her closet." I bent down and looked under the bed. There was nothing. I got my bat ready to attack anyone who might have been in the closet. I jerked the door open, but there was no one there. Miracle stopped growling and shaking. I said, "I guess it was just someone passing through." I went back to bed, and Miracle stayed on the bed with me until his mom got home.

I met Jeff Cox and moved to Big Sandy, Tennessee. There was one thing spooky in that trailer; I would be woken early in the morning by voices and music that sounded like they were coming from a radio. I couldn't make out what the voices were saying; the music sounded very old. We had no radio.

About a year later, Misty moved to Big Sandy. She stayed with us until she could get her own place, and she too heard the eerie radio station. It wasn't long before she met and married Andy Berry. Misty and I were so happy, and everything was going great for us.

Lane moved to the Autumn Pointe apartments in Sheffield. In a couple of weeks, I went to Lane's to visit for a few days to try to help her get through the move and the lonely days she was experiencing. I could tell she cherished the days we had and dreaded the day I would have to leave.

One chilly but sunny day, we decided to take a walk. Lane asked a man walking toward us, "Hello. How are you?" He didn't say a word; he just disappeared. Lane said, "How rude!" to him. She told me, "That man just disappeared."

I looked behind us and said, "Yep, he disappeared. He isn't here."

We finished our walk and returned to the apartment. "You just told a ghost how rude he was. I hope he doesn't decide to pay you a visit," I said with a chuckle.

That night, I wanted to sleep on the sofa with the TV going, so Lane went to her bed and fell asleep watching her TV. I was awakened by a very strange noise and Lane yelling, "Sheila! Help me!" I ran to her room, but the noise had stopped. I asked, "What was that weird sound?"

She could hardly speak, but through her trembling voice, she said, "It was my bed. It was shaking violently."

We spent the rest of the night on the sofa.

The day came, and we had to say our sad goodbyes. I hugged Lane and told her I would visit again as soon as I could. She held my hand as she walked me to the car. We hugged our last hug, and then I left my precious sister.

I had hoped the children and grandchildren wouldn't have these weird things happening, but they are still going on.

CHAPTER 12

Kissed by an Angel

by Misty Berry, Lane's Niece

I never knew my grandfather, Red, but I heard what a good man he had been to my grandmother, mom, my aunts, and the whole family. My mom had always told me she felt that I had been kissed by an angel when my Aunt Lane saw a shadowy figure come into the bedroom, lean over me while I was in my crib, and leave the room.

I was very close to my memaw. I loved her so much, and she loved me a lot too. She visited us often when we lived in Chattanooga. After I started school and we would get out for the summer, she would talk my mom into putting me on a bus by myself to spend the summer with her. Mom would get me on the bus, speak with the driver, and make sure I had the seat right behind him. There was no changing of buses between Chattanooga and Sheffield, Alabama, where Memaw would pick me up. We would get to her house and call my mom to let her know I had made it fine. Mom would call often to speak to us.

Memaw bought me a bicycle so I could go bike riding as long as I stayed close by. I had a lot of fun staying with Memaw. She would take me out to eat, take me to the park, and take me to visit my cousins. I think I filled a void in her life.

Memaw was getting sick during the last summer I spent with her. She started sending me on my bike to the grocery store with a list and money. The store was about four blocks away. The people there knew Memaw and me, so they would take my list, get the items, put the change in an envelope, and send me on my way.

After Memaw got sick, she sold her house and moved into an apartment. Mom moved us back to Alabama into the same apartment complex so we could be close to her. I got to visit her every day.

Then the day came that she had to go to the hospital and stay.

At that time, the hospitals didn't allow children to visit, but Mom took me over there a couple of times. One day, Mom came home from the hospital crying and told my brother, Jim, and me that Memaw had died and had gone to live with Jesus. I was devastated. I had just lost one of the most important persons in my life.

At the cemetery, we sat in front of the casket. I was in Mom's lap, and Jim was sitting next to us. When the preacher started saying the final words, I yelled, "I want to go with Memaw!"

Mom said, "Honey, you can't go. Memaw is in heaven." She held me tightly as I reached my arms out hoping Memaw would come out of that box and take me.

Our lives went on. Years passed. I got married and was soon expecting our first baby. We were staying with Mom, so my husband and I checked on a three-bedroom mobile home to buy. We loved it, but it was a little out of our price range unless we talked Mom and Jim into moving in with us. We talked it over with her, and she said okay. We all moved in and were getting along great.

A couple of weeks later, I went into labor and had a beautiful baby boy we named Aaron. The day I brought him home, I felt that someone was always watching me. I was still swollen from the birth. I was so glad my mom was there to help me.

Because my hands would swell at night, I would take my rings off and lay them in my tray on the bar in the kitchen. Even though the others would be at work during the day, I still felt that someone was watching me.

One morning, I woke up, and my rings were on my hand; my fingers had swollen around my wedding rings and Memaw's ring, which I had worn since Memaw's death. I thought maybe I had forgotten to take them off.

The next night, I made sure I took my rings off and put them in my tray, but the next morning, my rings were on my fingers. I was sure that someone in that house had to be playing a trick on me and I was going to find out who it was when they all got home.

Our dog started acting funny that day going from room to room and performing some tricks I didn't know he knew how to do. He was looking up and barking as if someone was telling him to bark.

Every time my baby cried, I would go to his room and pass the baby swing my mom had given me for my baby shower. It would start swinging even though I never got close to it. I just thought maybe the floor wasn't level.

When my husband got home from work, I told him about the strange happenings. He said, "I promise you I'm not pulling a joke on you."

I said, "Well, it must be Jim then because I don't believe Mom would do that."

When Mom and Jim came in, I started fussing at Jim for playing such a dirty trick on me, but he said, "It wasn't me."

Right then, the swing started swinging, and it swung for a minute. "That's another thing," I said looking at my husband. "You need to level this floor so that swing won't do that."

Later after supper, I told them, "I'm taking my rings off and putting them in my tray. No one better touch them." I washed the dishes and got ready for bed. I was exhausted. I gave my baby a bath and told them I was going to bed.

It didn't take me long to fall asleep, but something woke me up about two; I felt my hand being touched. I sat up ready to argue with someone, but there was Memaw, and I could see through her. The dog woke up at that time and started barking at Memaw so loudly that it woke everyone up. The dog went into the living room, so my husband and I got up and went too. Mom and Jim came to the living room too wondering what was wrong.

I couldn't see Memaw anymore. The dog started doing tricks in the living room. He would roll over, play dead, and shake hands, and he would look up at something that wasn't there. I said to them, "I saw Memaw. She put the rings on my fingers."

All of a sudden, the dog was scratching roughly on the door to go out. I let him out, and he started doing tricks outside. We all were watching this strange behavior. The dog reached out his paw, barked one last bark, and came in the house. We watched him in amazement. Mom said to me, "I bet Mother came back to see your baby and then let us know she was leaving."

The dog never did another trick no matter how hard we tried to get him to, the swing didn't swing by itself anymore, and my rings stayed in my tray at night. I hoped that was the last time that I would see a ghost, but it wasn't.

A few years later, I got a divorce, and Aaron and I moved to Leighton, a small town close to the Shoals area. I rented a little house by the elementary school. One night after putting my son to bed, I decided to watch some TV. I passed the bathroom and saw that the light was still on even though I thought I had turned it off. I looked in to see if Aaron had gotten up to use the bathroom, but he wasn't in there. I turned the light off, checked on Aaron, who was still in bed, and went to the living room. I heard a noise coming from the hallway. I didn't see anything, but I could tell the bathroom light was on again, so I went to check on Aaron. He was still asleep. I went in the bathroom and unscrewed the light bulb. I made a mental note to call the landlord to check it out.

I went back to the living room to finish watching my movie. When it was over, I was going to my bedroom and the bathroom light was on again. Someone or something was playing tricks on me because the bulb had been screwed back into the socket.

I searched the entire house making sure all doors and windows were securely locked. I found nothing.

The next evening after work and after picking up Aaron from the sitter, we got a pizza and headed home. We pulled into the driveway, and since it was dusk, I could see that the bathroom light was on through the small bathroom window. We had been in a hurry that morning, so maybe I had left it on I thought.

We ate our pizza, and I gave Aaron his bath and got him ready for bed. I was taking a bath when the light went out. I yelled, "Aaron, turn the light back on, and don't turn it off again when I'm in here."

Aaron came to the bathroom and said, "Mommy, I didn't turn it off."

I finished my bath and put my pajamas on. I went to check on Aaron. I said, "Aaron honey, I'm sorry I yelled at you. I love you, baby." He said, "I love you Mommy." Then I kissed him goodnight and tucked him in.

By that time, I knew what it was and was glad I hadn't called the landlord. She would have thought I was nuts. I continued to stay there, and the bathroom light continued coming on and going off.

It wasn't long before I started dating again, fell in love, married again, moved again, and was expecting my second baby. I had another little boy I named Dylan. A couple of years passed, and I knew I couldn't stay with this husband either. I started applying for apartments back in the Tuscumbia area.

I got a call from Ivy Point Apartments, a new apartment complex I had applied for an apartment at. I was so happy; these apartments had a great yard for the children to play in. I leased a three-bedroom apartment so Aaron and Dylan would have their own rooms. Life would be good again, or so I thought.

Things were nice and peaceful for a few months. Then one night after we were all in bed, the TV came on. It was on the Nickelodeon channel, and the volume was increasing as I walked toward it. It woke both boys up, and they came to the living room asking what it was. I turned it off and told them that it was a new TV that something must have been set on it to come on at a certain time. That seemed to please them, and we all went back to bed.

The next evening after work, I looked through the manual, but there was no alarm you could set on this TV. *Oh no,* I thought. *Here we go again.* I unplugged the TV, locked the door, and went to bed.

At three in the morning, a small noise woke me up. I got up and went to the living room. I couldn't believe what I was seeing. The TV was on, but it was all static. It was still unplugged. I pushed the off button, and it went off. I went back to bed.

The next morning, I got the boys up a few minutes early to clean their rooms since it was inspection day. I promised to take them to the park if they did a good job. They did well, so after I got off work, we went to the park. When I got home, I found a note the manager had left me; she needed to see me. I got the boys settled down and told them I was going to see the manager for just a minute. She lived a couple of apartments down.

I went into the office to see what she wanted. She said that she had gone into my apartment to do the inspection with the maintenance man and that the TV had come on by itself. She had pushed the off button but it hadn't gone off. She reached down to unplug it and saw that it was already unplugged. That terrified her so badly that she said the maintenance men would inspect my apartment from then on. She said that she had a very eerie feeling when she went into my apartment that had almost made her sick.

Mother came to visit the next day, and as we were sitting and talking about the TV, a toy police car started coming toward us with the siren going. At first, Mom thought one of us had sat on a remote control. I told her that the car wasn't remote control, it was battery operated, but there were no batteries in it. The toy car ran into her foot, so she bent over and picked it up. She opened up the battery slot and saw that it was empty. She asked me, "Do you have any idea who it may be?"

"I think it might be a young boy," I said.

Dylan had seen a young boy across the street by the telephone pole as we were leaving one morning. He asked, "Mom, who is that?"

"Who, Dylan?" I asked.

"That boy right there," he said pointing at the telephone pole.

"Honey, I don't see a little boy," I said.

We got in the car and started out of the parking lot. As we were going past the telephone pole, Dylan asked, "Do you see the little boy waving?"

Dylan was waving back, but I still didn't see anything, so I just said, "Oh, okay."

The TV kept coming on, the toys kept racing across the floor, and I heard a child laughing. I assumed it was the little boy Dylan had seen that day by the telephone pole. It was driving me crazy, so I thought another move was in the works so I wouldn't lose my mind.

I met one of my old school friends, Jason, and we started going out. I finally told him about the things going on in the apartment. He looked at me disbelievingly, but he didn't laugh at me or judge me. He came over to watch a movie one evening, and we settled down on the couch with popcorn and sodas. The boys lay on the carpet with their popcorn and drinks. About fifteen minutes into the movie, the TV started showing static on the screen and the child's laughter was heard by us all. I told him, "I'm so sorry, but it looks like it's going to be one of those nights."

He looked at the connections on the TV and DVR but couldn't find any reason for the TV messing up like that. I had another TV in Aaron's room, so I got that. It was small, but we did get to finish watching the movie.

Jason said, "I better go. I have a long day at work tomorrow."

I walked him to the door, and as he started to kiss me goodnight, the toy police car came from the kitchen racing toward us. It rammed into Jason's shoe. He said, "I hate that you're living with a ghost. I think we ought to move in together and get you out of here. On second thought, since we've been friends forever, why don't we just get married, find us a new mobile home, and move it to my land on Underwood Mountain?"

"You know what, Jason? I think we could make that work," I said.

We got married in two weeks. We purchased a beautiful three-bedroom mobile home and moved to the mountain about twelve miles from Tuscumbia. The boys loved it. There was a fishing pond behind us on Jason's mother's land, so the boys learned to fish, and they loved the place. We had a pool table that was lots of fun for young and old. We had several family parties, and it seemed that everyone always had a good time. It was nice and peaceful.

One day, I was cleaning my kitchen and heard voices, but they were not quite loud enough for me to tell what they were saying. I knew there wasn't anyone home but me, so I peeked out of the window thinking I might see some people outside, but there was no one. I turned around and saw three dark shadows coming out of the living room and going into my bedroom. "Oh, dear Lord, not again!" I exclaimed.

Jason came in from work, kissed me, and headed into our bedroom to take a shower in the back bathroom. I didn't tell him what I had heard or seen.

The next week, Deedra came to visit. We were talking and laughing when suddenly Deedra stopped and had a strange look on her face. I asked, "What's wrong, Dee?"

She just pointed, and I turned to look in the direction she was pointing, and there were these dark forms coming out of the living room and going into my bedroom. I told her that I had seen them the previous week and had heard voices I hadn't been able to make out what they were saying.

"Do you think these things happen only in our family?" she asked.

"I don't think so, but I sure don't like it. It happens too often for me. I wished it would leave me alone," I answered.

I told her I wasn't going to tell Jason and asked her not to either if she should happen to run into him. She said she wouldn't, and we talked a while longer before she had to leave.

Jason came home from work one afternoon, and another car followed him into the driveway. There was a girl in the car, and I saw him lean down and kiss her. I was hurt and mad. We had just celebrated our sixth anniversary. I asked him about the girl, and he said, "I may as well tell you that I've been seeing her."

Here we go again, I thought. Another move was going to be necessary.

Aaron had gone to stay with his dad and Dylan went to stay with his dad, so I got a job working at a plant at Hackleberg, Alabama, and got my boys on the weekends. I met a good friend at the plant, and she said I could be her roommate. She lived in Hackleberg, which was about a fifty-minute drive from Tuscumbia. She gave me the bedroom at one end of the home, which had a bathroom; I fixed up another bedroom for the boys. She also told me I could have a dog, so I bought a Shih Tzu puppy and named him Miracle.

I had fun decorating the bedrooms, and I kept their bedroom door closed. One morning as I was getting ready for work, I noticed that the bedroom door was open. I thought maybe my roommate had gone in there for some reason and decided to ask her about it when we came home from work.

When she got home, she said that she had not gone in there. I tried to forget about it and play with my little dog. She was sitting on the couch and I was in the floor when we heard a creaking sound. My roommate got up and came back and said, "That door just opened," referring to the door of the boy's bedroom. She said she didn't know why it had started opening. I was sure hoping I didn't know the reason, so I just said, "Maybe the mobile home is unbalanced a little from the heavy winds we've been having."

"That's a possibility. I'll have a friend of mine come check it out," she said.

Right after she said that, my puppy, Miracle, went to the hallway and started barking in front of the boys' bedroom as if he could see someone. I jumped up and went to pick him up, and Melanie said, "Something's not normal about this. I think we may have a ghost."

"A ghost?" I asked.

"It's possible," she said.

So we put up with the bedroom door opening and closing and would tell the boys the trailer wasn't level.

One evening, we came home after supper at the local diner. I headed toward my bedroom and noticed a glow coming from my room. I yelled for Melanie. We peeked in the door not knowing what to expect, and we saw a transparent young boy sitting on my dresser. I grabbed my camera out of my pocket and took a picture of the little boy before he faded away. "Did you see that?" I asked.

"I sure did. I saw that little boy. You may have gotten a good picture of him before he disappeared," she said.

My hands were shaking, but I looked at my picture and could barely see his image.

I went to visit Mom and showed her the picture. She could see the little boy. "I bet that little boy from the apartments has followed you all these years and is now letting you know he's there." I told her about a ball bouncing in the kitchen that had woken both of us, but when we would go look, the ball would be still.

I decided to move again when I got the job at a doctor's office in Sheffield, Alabama; I found an apartment close to the office. My mom had moved back from Idaho and was looking for an apartment too. I told her we could be roommates, and she said, "Good idea."

The apartment had two bedrooms, and it was good to have company. Mom would take Miracle on a walk every day; they were getting along great. She had told me about the tall man in dark clothing and the old music she had heard. I had heard the music but had not seen the man up to that point.

After we had lived there a few months, Mom went to bed early one night, and it was a quiet night, so I decided to take my bath a little early. I put some bath gel in the tub, turned on my radio to country music at a low volume, and folded up a towel for a pillow. I got in the tub, lay back in the warm water, and shut my eyes. It was nice. Then suddenly Mom was yelling at me on the other side of the door. "Misty! Misty! Are you all right?" she screamed.

"Yes, Mom. What's wrong?"

I grabbed a towel to put around me and noticed the doorknob

turning back and forth real fast. I said, "Mom, quit turning the doorknob."

"I'm not touching it," she said. "I see it, but I'm not touching it. I heard you screaming for me."

"It wasn't me, Mom," I said.

"Misty, I'm opening the door." She barged in. "It felt like someone holding the door and then just letting go. Are you sure you're okay?"

"I'm okay, just still shaking from getting scared," I said.

"I heard you scream like you were hurt, and then I saw the doorknob doing that turning thing. Then I felt something pushing me. That was scary."

"But Mom, it wasn't me screaming," I said.

Mom said, "May be a warning!"

A couple of years went by, and Mom had met a very nice man and had moved to Big Sandy, Tennessee.

Later in the year, I needed some help and called Mom. She just said, "Get your rear end up here." When I got up there, I went out job hunting the next day and got a job. I cried every night for a while because I was missing my friends back home in Alabama, but I was making friends in Big Sandy.

I finally met Andy Berry, fell in love, and got married. He has helped me acquire my dream of being a race car driver, which I had wanted since I was young. I told him I wanted to have my own business, and he built me a corner in his big heavy equipment shop, and I loved it.

I decided that the Camden area would be better for me to sell my homemade soy candles and Bath & Body products so I saved my money and found a place. Andy helped me move my shop. He had gotten hurt in August when a tree came through the window of the loader he was operating and pinned him down for five hours with a limb stuck through him. He was air-flighted to Vanderbilt Hospital and was there for a few days. He was not able to work for a few months. We were not sure how we were going to make our finances work out, but we knew we were going to do this together.

The community came together with an event in his name; friends and family wanted to make donations, dinners were delivered, and family and friends would take us to eat after Andy was able. Later, I found a bigger shop in the town square, and Andy helped me move again.

Mother and I are living peacefully except for some really old music that plays every now and then at her house with no radio or TV on, and others have heard it too.

Another time at Mother's, I had come to pick up my TV, and while I was putting it in the car, something came from under the car and grabbed my legs. I put the TV down and kicked off the ugly hands holding my legs and ran in Mom's shaking terribly. I stayed and calmed down for a while. I told her I would be okay, and she walked me out to my car.

Things have gotten better for Mother and me. I was hoping my offspring wouldn't have such things to bother them, but they both already have stories they can tell.

ABOUT THE AUTHOR

Ruby Aline "Lane" Baker was born at home in Tuscumbia, a small town in Alabama. She was the third daughter of Mr. and Mrs. Clay Howard. Her happy home was turned upside down when she lost her father when she was six. She started seeing and hearing things that others could not see or hear.

As she got older, some of these things became terrifying, and some of these experiences could be heard by others. This book tells about some of those experiences.

Seeing things that others can't is terribly confusing to a young child. Realizing you are different causes problems that no child should have to face. He or she learns to stay quiet about seeing ghosts or spirits and to talk only to loved ones who understand what is going on.

As I got older, the ghosts seemed to become scarier, and some were violent. My husband had his doubts about my ghosts until he started experiencing some of the ghostly things with me.

I hope this book will help those who see things and let them know they are not alone or insane.

Printed in the United States
By Bookmasters